PEER TUTORING

A Teacher's Resource Guide

Edward E. Gordon

ScarecrowEducation
Lanham, Maryland • Toronto • Oxford
2005

Published in the United States of America
by ScarecrowEducation
An imprint of The Rowman & Littlefield Publishing Group, Inc.
4501 Forbes Boulevard, Suite 200, Lanham, Maryland 20706
www.scarecroweducation.com

PO Box 317
Oxford
OX2 9RU, UK

British Library Cataloguing in Publication Information Available

Library of Congress Cataloging-in-Publication Data
Gordon, Edward E.
   Peer tutoring : a teacher's resource guide / Edward E. Gordon.
     p. cm.
   Includes bibliographical references.
   ISBN 1-57886-173-X (pbk. : alk. paper)
   1. Peer-group tutoring of students—Handbooks, manuals, etc. I. Title.
  LB1031.5.G67 2005
  371.39'4—dc22
                        2004020471

∞™ The paper used in this publication meets the minimum requirements of American National Standard for
Information Sciences—Permanence of Paper for Printed Library Materials, ANSI/NISO Z39.48-1992.
Manufactured in the United States of America.

CONTENTS

List of Figures   v

List of Tables   vii

Foreword   ix

Acknowledgments   xi

Introduction   xiii

1   What Is Peer Tutoring?   1

2   Defining and Planning a Peer Tutoring Program   7

3   Training Peer Tutors: "People Learn While They Teach"   13

4   Training Program Case Studies: "To Teach Is to Learn Twice"   27

5   Assessment and Evaluation   49

6   Success Stories: "The IQ Is Often Less Important in Any Person's Education Than the I Will!"   67

7   Finding Long-Term Support   75

Bibliography   79

About the Author   81

LIST OF FIGURES

Figure 2.1.	Sample Permission Form for Tutors	9
Figure 2.2.	Sample Permission Form for Tutees	10
Figure 3.1.	Flowchart of the Peer Tutor Training Program	14
Figure 3.2.	Example of Tutor Diary	16
Figure 3.3.	Example of Tutoring Class Report	17
Figure 3.4.	A Job Aid for Tutors	18
Figure 3.5.	Example of Stimulus-Response Instructional Outcomes—Preschool	18
Figure 3.6.	Example of Stimulus-Response Instructional Outcomes—Primary Grades	19
Figure 3.7.	Classroom Observation by Student for Cross-Age Tutor Training	22
Figure 4.1.	Steps for Tutors to Use in a Session	28
Figure 4.2.	Tutor Tips: Tutoring Session Management	29
Figure 4.3.	Tutor Log (Case Study 1)	31
Figure 4.4.	Format for Daily Peer Quiz	32
Figure 4.5.	Format for Fact Test	34
Figure 4.6.	Sample Feeling Card	35
Figure 4.7.	Setting Objectives	36
Figure 4.8.	Sample Chart for Skills Mastery Sequences	38
Figure 4.9.	Example of a Flash Card Scoring Sheet	39
Figure 4.10.	Tutor Log (Case Study 4)	43
Figure 4.11.	Basic Competency Spelling List	46
Figure 4.12.	Spelling Data Sheet	47
Figure 5.1.	Tutor Guide	51
Figure 5.2.	Tutor Observation Checklist	52
Figure 5.3.	Sample Tutor Skills Checklist	53
Figure 5.4.	Sample Tutor Summary Report Form	54
Figure 5.5a.	Sample Parent Short-Term Evaluation of Tutoring Program	57
Figure 5.5b.	Sample Parent Long-Term Evaluation of Tutoring Program	59
Figure 5.6a.	Sample Teacher Short-Term Evaluation of Tutoring Program	61
Figure 5.6b.	Sample Teacher Long-Term Evaluation of Tutoring Program	63

LIST OF TABLES

Table I.1. Differences between Classroom Teaching and Tutoring   xiv

Table 5.1. Outline of a Plan for the Evaluation of a Tutoring Program   56

FOREWORD

The No Child Left Behind (NCLB) Act of 2001 requires universal student achievement of state standards. A strength of NCLB is its challenge to educators to confront disparities in student achievement. A weakness is NCLB's assumption that improvement of student learning is continuous and consistent and can be accomplished in a fixed amount of time—regardless of a student's starting place (Rose, 2004). To meet the challenge of NCLB, teachers increasingly face the instructional dilemma of bringing whole groups of students "to standard" on high-stakes tests while finding ways to individualize instruction to meet the needs of students whose performance is not continuous or consistent.

Successful learning depends on a constant flow of information that helps students not only to check on their learning but also to improve it. Teachers can help students understand the achievement targets they need to hit. Teachers can use classroom activities and assessments to build students' confidence in themselves as learners, provide students with constructive guidance and frequent feedback, adjust instruction to meet students' needs, and engage students in self-assessment and self-management. This can, however, sometimes feel like a daunting responsibility. *Peer Tutoring: A Teacher's Resource Guide* provides teachers with a clear, concise, research-based view of the potential role that peer tutoring can play in helping teachers meet the challenge of successful student learning.

Peer tutoring as a learning strategy provides tutees with reinforcement of teacher instruction. Tutors reinforce concepts, help tutees practice skills, assist with individual projects, support problem solving, or challenge tutees' thinking or approaches to learning. Peer tutoring also strengthens tutors' understanding of concepts and skills, engages them in creative thinking and problem solving as they work to support tutees, and enhances tutors' self-image. *Peer Tutoring* provides a compelling argument for the contribution of peer tutoring not only to increased mastery of knowledge and skills but also to student motivation and empowerment as learners.

The use of peer tutors in classrooms opens opportunities for teachers to observe students more closely and gain more detailed understanding of individual students' learning profiles and mastery of concepts and skills. Peer tutoring makes it possible to embed assessments of knowledge and skill in learning activities, giving teachers multiple ways to monitor and check student progress. Finally, peer tutoring can provide valuable time for teachers to work more closely with individual students needing reteaching or greater support in practicing less-developed skills.

Peer Tutoring makes it clear that effective peer tutoring requires careful planning and is grounded in appropriate training of tutors. Effective peer tutoring is not a haphazard volunteer program. Peer tutoring requires a purposeful program of specific learning objectives, activities, and assessments for developing and determining students' mastery of concepts and skills. To be effective tutors, students need to learn how to interact with peers as "learning partners." The author points out that peer tutors are more successful if their role is highly structured, if they are made aware of basic learning principles, if they understand curricular goals, and if they are trained in the appropriate use of tutoring activities and materials.

Peer Tutoring does not ignore or dismiss the potential hurdles that teachers will face as they consider the utility of peer tutoring in their classrooms. The author also wisely cautions that peer tutoring will require parent and organizational support. Parents generally know very little about peer tutoring; they need to be educated about the role of peer tutoring as a support and supplement to teacher instruction and the benefits of tutoring both for the tutee and the tutor.

The author provides a credible argument that peer tutoring has positive effects not only on student learning, but also on student motivation and the general classroom climate. These additional payoffs from peer tutoring are good news both to parents and school administrators. *Peer Tutoring's* attention to the importance of assessing learning, student progress, tutor effectiveness, and overall program results provides guidance for teachers regarding the kind of information that can be gathered and communicated to garner administrative and community support.

The strength of *Peer Tutoring* comes from Ed Gordon's firsthand expertise and rich experience as a tutor, as the founder and CEO of a tutoring service, as a developer of tutor training and curriculum guides, and as a researcher of the history, conduct, and impact of tutoring on learners of all ages, both in schools and in work settings. *Peer Tutoring* provides descriptive case studies as examples of the application of theory to practice, clear explanations of research on peer tutoring, and an array of tools that teachers can use to guide their initiation, development, and assessment of a classroom peer tutoring program. Simply stated, Ed Gordon knows his stuff, and his passion for the contributions that peer tutoring can make to learner success is unabashedly obvious.

Peer Tutoring: A Teacher's Resource Guide does indeed offer teachers a "fresh examination" of peer and cross-age tutoring and their potential to support individual student learning needs and improve student learning. But, *Peer Tutoring* also speaks to teachers on a different level. Research on the impact of high-stakes testing on classroom instruction provides examples of teaching and learning approaches that are often discontinued to focus on high-stakes testing (e.g., Abrams, Pedulla, & Madaus, 2003; Barksdale-Ladd & Thomas, 2000; Herman & Golan, 1991; Johnston, 1998; McNeil, 2000; Smith, 1991). Teachers report spending more time on test preparation and less time on learning activities that provide reinforcement of skills, promote in-depth understanding of content, involve collaboration as well as independence, and invoke higher order thinking skills (Barksdale-Ladd & Thomas, 2000).

Ed Gordon knows from firsthand experience and research that peer tutoring can provide an opportunity for teachers and students to bring greater reinforcement, student-centered support, peer collaboration, and creative problem solving back into test-driven classrooms. *Peer Tutoring* provides a clear and engaging perspective that helps teachers to understand the potential of peer tutoring for reconfirming the principles of good learning and assessment and for reconnecting teachers to students, and students to students, as partners in learning.

Judith A. Ponticell
Professor and Chair
Educational Leadership and Policy Studies
College of Education
University of South Florida
Tampa

ACKNOWLEDGMENTS

Many individuals and organizations have contributed over the years to the ideas presented in *Peer Tutoring: A Teacher's Resource Guide*. This includes other researchers at many universities across the United States and hundreds of classroom teachers. They include Ronald R. Morgan, Loyola University, Chicago; Judith A. Ponticell, University of South Florida; Frances Ryan, DePaul University; Eunice Askov, Pennsylvania State University; Hans Schieser, DePaul University; Douglas G. Ellson; Mary McNeil Pierce; Kristina Stahlbrand; Suzanne Bryant Armstrong; and many other professional educators.

In particular, I again offer my deepest thanks to Sandra Gula, who has once again done an outstanding job in helping to prepare the final manuscript. Above all others, my wife and colleague, Elaine Gordon, has applied her editing and research expertise as a professional librarian, writer, and editor to greatly improve the final product.

However, for any errors or shortcomings the reader may find, the author takes sole responsibility.

Edward E. Gordon
Chicago, Illinois

INTRODUCTION

In this era of high-stakes testing, teachers across America are struggling with the demands of increasingly standardized curricula. They, in turn, are being linked to the use of standardized achievement tests to assess student, teacher, and school performance.

The passage of the No Child Left Behind (NCLB) Act of 2001 has raised this standards movement to an even higher level. In part, these increased academic demands stem from technological, economic, and social forces that are changing America and the entire world.

Teachers need a fresh examination of what we know about using meaningful learning approaches and strategies that consistently cultivate deeper understandings in (or between) learners. A host of labels have been used to describe these general teaching approaches: teaching for understanding, teaching for meaning, child-centered teaching, or transformative teaching, to mention a few.

The purpose of *Peer Tutoring: A Teacher's Resource Guide* is to give teachers specific methods that will help more students construct better personal meaning from their classroom learning (i.e., constructivism). We review the rich case study histories of peer and cross-age tutoring in which many teachers have already successfully implemented many prescriptive instructional principles.

In some of my previous books, I have investigated the background and methods of tutors in America and Europe. This research explored the educational work not just of adult teachers, but often of student peer tutors. From this information and my own long-term field research gained through founding and heading a tutoring service, I have attempted to explicate the major differences between classroom teaching and tutoring (see Table I.1).

While studying the tutoring needs of both children and adult learners, my colleagues and I developed tutor-training procedures to retrain teachers as tutors. At the same time, we investigated the rich published literature on contemporary peer tutoring and developed teacher workshops to help schools begin their own classroom programs. This book is the long-term result of these efforts.

Students today have a whole new world of information, ideas, and experiences accessed through the Internet. What most teachers lack are successful ways of framing the art of teaching to take advantage of this new resource-rich environment. Peer tutoring helps teachers co-construct knowledge with students to help classroom learning become more student centered, or child centered. It can become an important learning element that assists the student in learning how to solve problems, collaborate with others, think creatively—all part of the critical-thinking process so important for students to master because a greater percentage of high school graduates will probably enroll in some form of postsecondary education.

Table I.1 Differences between Classroom Teaching and Tutoring

Classroom Teaching	Tutoring
Large group of students	One-to-one or very small group (up to 5)
Group instruction	Individualized Learning
Generalized group learning needs	Precise diagnosis of individual learning needs
Student learning styles only generalized	Individual's learning styles precisely defined
Teaching to group needs	Prescriptive tutoring
Learning paced by the group's ability	Learning paced by individual's ability
Learning materials selected for entire group	Learning materials selected for individual's interests and needs
Motivation to learn dominated by the group	Individual can be more easily motivated to learn
Learning curve controlled by group's progress	Learning curve controlled by individual's progress
Learning results averaged for group	Learning results can be accelerated for the individual

Source: Gordon, *Tutor Quest*

In some ways, all of these ideas have been tried before by teachers struggling to implement the ideas of the progressive educators. Francis Parker at Chicago's Normal School, John Dewey at the University of Chicago Laboratory School, and many others championed child-centered approaches based on the earlier theories of Rousseau, Froebel, and Pestalozzi.

Historian Lawrence Cremin, in his analysis of educational reforms, believes that this progressive education required "infinitely skilled teachers." They would create curricula adapted to the needs of learners, manage more student-active classrooms, and creatively assess student learning. Unfortunately, then as now, all these demands have usually overwhelmed most teachers.

One of the chief obstacles is the difficulty in overcoming the entrenched culture of "schooling." The predominant images of "being students and teacher" can be best summed up by the medieval monastery rule, "It belongeth to the master to speak and to teach; it becometh the disciple to be silent and to listen."

Recent studies show that most teachers, administrators, and parents expect an effective classroom to be quiet and orderly. Students are seated and not talking to each other. By maintaining this discipline, teachers control the intellectual activity and expose all the students in a uniform way to the curriculum. Students are trained to become passive observers rather than active participants in their own education. Most teachers were themselves taught in such a traditional classroom of teacher-centered instruction, fact-based subject matter, and drill and practice.

It is not very surprising that most teachers are not guided by current critical-thinking instructional models, but by the powerful mental models of teaching that shaped their own behavior as students. Other community members are also very suspicious of the teaching methods that are different from those they remember as part of their own schooling experiences. Instead, we have the public calling for "back to basics," "real," or "fundamental" education. The recent increased interest in preserving or studying one-room schools is perhaps part of this yearning to go back to "authentic education practices."

Yet the example of one-room schooling makes an interesting case for some of the student-centered learning practices we review here. Recent historical documentation shows that since the children in these one-room schools were often at such different educational levels and ages, teachers found they could not do the entire instructional job alone. They used peer tutors and cross-age tutors. The consensus among teachers and parents alike was that this method helped the tutee's education and simultaneously strengthened the learning and self-image of the tutor. Peer tutors gave teachers more time to work with students individually and also obtain a detailed understanding of each student's learning style and degree of subject mastery. The effective use of peer tutoring in one-room schools across America helped create a familiar, child-centered classroom environment and acted as an "instructional secret" that helped make one-room schooling a success story for so many students.

For peer tutoring to be effective, historical and contemporary research has found that teachers must develop strategies for socializing students into new ways of interacting with peers as learning partners. Students require training to become effective peer or cross-age tutors to avoid negative behaviors such as bickering, demeaning comments, exclusion, or academic freeloading. Training also helps overcome the indifference of capable students in potentially helping their peers.

Peer tutoring can provide teachers useful assistance in observing where learners are in the developmental process. This gives teachers a unique opportunity because careful observation of a student's day-to-day learning is rarely available in the typical American classroom. Using peer tutoring, the teacher can both observe effective learning models in action and coach the tutor to improve the learning performance of his or her tutee. Finally, peer tutoring programs can be grounded in meaningful contexts that offer assessment opportunities to determine the overall excellence of classroom learning. These are not pre/post-standardized tests. Instead, peer tutoring offers assessment methods embedded in the learning activities themselves. These may include student journals, tutor diaries, observation reports, interviewing, peer reviews, criterion-referenced quizzes, and tests—to mention a few.

In *Peer Tutoring: A Teacher's Resource Guide*, some of the practical learning issues we review are:

- Why is peer/cross-age tutoring an important practice?
- In what classroom contexts might tutoring be useful?
- Who are the student populations that have benefited from it?
- Where can it be done?
- When are these programs provided?
- How does peer/cross-age tutoring broaden the assessment of learning?

Chapter 1, "What Is Peer Tutoring?" gives teachers an overview of its origins and why peer tutoring has proven so effective. It also begins to address the traditional objections from educators and parents that peer tutoring takes time away from traditional instruction.

"Defining and Planning a Peer Tutoring Program," chapter 2, provides teachers with the five essential steps to follow when designing a classroom program. Proper planning saves both the overall time invested in a peer tutoring program and helps avoid later frustration by steering clear of these most common curriculum and administrative errors.

Student training is the single-most important component in any peer tutoring program. Chapter 3, "Training Peer Tutors: People Learn While They Teach," presents several different tutor-training programs for teachers to consider using. These models include peer, cross-age, and high school programs.

Chapter 4, "Training Program Case Studies: To Teach Is to Learn Twice," offers a broad selection of training case studies. It reviews the program setting, rationale for tutoring, pretesting, choosing the tutors, training sessions content, tutoring session methods, monitoring procedures, and program evaluation. Published research offers teachers a broad array of training methods that have proven successful in programs across the United States.

Chapter 5, "Assessment and Evaluation," presents information on avoiding the second major reason that peer tutoring fails. It covers the content of a meaningful daily assessment of the tutor activity. What information will be useful to conduct tutor retraining? How will the teacher conduct both the short-term and long-term evaluation of results?

Over forty years of research provides a literature rich in success stories. Ordinary teachers have profitably used these programs. Chapter 6, "Success Stories: The IQ Is Often Less Important in Any Person's Education Than the I Will!" presents overviews from a wide variety of elementary, high school, college, peer, and cross-age tutoring programs.

"Finding Long-Term Support" is the focus of chapter 7. In order to sustain a peer tutoring program, you the teacher will need to motivate administrators, other teachers, parents, students, and yourself. This final chapter reviews strategies that have been used to retain and increase support for peer tutoring programs.

Peer Tutoring: A Teacher's Resource Guide provides sample peer tutoring materials developed by teachers. These forms will help save teachers time at the beginning of their program. The documents are also a good starting point to use your creativity to adapt and develop them for your own program. Additional references and resources are listed for those teachers who wish to explore for themselves the rich published literature on peer/cross-age tutoring.

WHAT IS PEER TUTORING?

He who teaches others, teaches himself.

—Comenius, 1632

The idea of students teaching other students is not a new concept discovered by twenty-first-century American educators. In ancient Rome, the philosopher Quintilian recommended a student tutor as a strong role model that a child will first strive "to imitate and then to outdo." Even earlier, ancient Hindu schools used mutual instruction of one student by another.

By the early 1800s, European schools also made widespread use of student tutors. Grammar schools in England, France, Germany, and elsewhere used this method, sometimes called "simultaneous instruction," "decurions," or the "monitorial system." However, they all relied upon a student tutor teaching a student tutee.

In the United States before 1920, the majority of children attended one-room schools. Children were at many different educational levels and ages. Teachers found they could not do the entire instructional job alone. Therefore, they used older students as tutors to help younger children or their own peer group. The consensus among educators and parents was that this method helped the younger child's education and simultaneously strengthened the learning and self-image of the older peer tutor. Time moved on. America urbanized. Large schools won out.

By the early 1960s, there was a revival of student tutoring. Volunteer tutors, classroom "pull-out" teachers acting as tutors, and a revival of student peer tutoring were employed as instructional methods to improve student classroom learning.

DEFINING PEER TUTORING

Peer tutoring is an instructional method in which one child tutors another in material on which the tutor is an "expert" and the tutee is a "novice." However, multiple definitions of peer tutoring exist.

To make matters more confusing, peer tutoring is often substituted for cross-age tutoring, in which an older student teaches a younger child. Many other descriptive terms have surfaced including: "peer teaching," "partner learning," "peer education," "child-teach-child," or "mutual instruction."

Here we only discuss peer tutoring in which one classroom student tutors another student in his or her same classroom or cross-age tutoring where an older student or an adult tutors a younger student

STRATEGIES FOR A PEER TUTORING PROGRAM

A successful peer-tutoring program uses six key strategies:

1. Defining and planning a peer tutoring program
2. Training peer tutors
3. Monitoring daily results
4. Assessing peer tutoring
5. Finding support for peer tutoring
6. Sustaining a peer tutoring program

Defining and Planning

At the core of any classroom peer tutoring program is determining the specific curriculum goals and objectives that a teacher wishes to achieve. Tutoring is meant to act as a supplemental learning strategy that reinforces the instructor's daily teaching. Peer tutoring can be used in almost any subject area, ranging from reading, social sciences, and writing to math and science. Peer tutoring can reinforce basic knowledge, practice skills, help with a student project, even provide enrichment, or act as a system to reward student achievement.

After selecting the subject area, the teacher needs to plan a peer tutoring program that will feature a precise format of student activities. This will guide the entire process from the beginning to the end of each tutoring session. Planning will range from how to select the first student tutors, set up a classroom tutoring environment, establish a tutoring plan of rules, regulations, and reports for students to follow and give special recognition for achievement.

Training

Teaching students usable peer tutoring methods is essential for the program's success. Not only does effective tutor training need to be conducted at the beginning of the program, but also it needs to be maintained for retraining purposes and to introduce new tutors to the classroom program. Lack of effective tutor training is the number-one cause of the ultimate failure of most classroom peer tutoring efforts. This can be easily avoided through short-term and long-term planning.

Monitoring and Assessment

Tutoring results can be determined using both formal and informal assessment tools. These include pretesting/posttesting; measuring a skill outcome before each class, based on the tutee's present knowledge; a daily progress report for parents; or tracking progress in completing an ongoing learning project, such as a science experiment. Teachers train tutors on how to use or sometimes even select from different meaningful assessment tools.

Finding Support

Once a teacher has decided to begin a classroom peer tutoring program, he or she will need support from three very different groups: the school's principal, the students, and the student's parents. Most principals will respond to the compelling peer tutoring research of the last twenty years. Research has shown that peer tutoring is a low-cost curriculum reinforcement program. It can significantly increase a student's learning. Peer tutoring can be used effectively by almost any teacher, right in the classroom.

For students, there are many strong motivators. These include:

1. A reward for high performing students who can become bored by the pace of instruction.
2. An independent activity that lets students "do their own thing" within the boundaries of the tutoring program.
3. Tutoring helps students admit in private to a peer that they "just don't get it." It allows the peer tutor to explain the solution in terms more understandable to a child or adolescent.
4. Eventually almost every student in a class will have the opportunity to assume the "tutor" role. For most students, this will be seen as an informal recognition of their personal success as a learner.

To receive parental support, teachers need to share the proven research results that all children can benefit through peer tutoring. "I send my child to school to be taught by a teacher, not to tutor someone else's child. He or she will miss out on valuable instruction," is the typical first reaction by many parents to a proposed classroom peer tutoring program. Parents need to be given understandable proof that, first, for the tutee, private instruction will help supplement the teacher's efforts so that the student will learn more in the classroom on a day-to-day basis. Second, for the tutor, research has clearly shown that "overlearning" usually results when a student assumes the role of a teacher. The tutor gains a more in-depth understanding of how to apply the skills and lessons he or she knows, or more creatively use the information he or she tutors. Tutoring can become a means of increasing a student's critical-thinking abilities.

Sustaining

Within the classroom, peer tutoring can help begin a personal recognition system of student achievement. Almost every student will want to become "certified" as a peer tutor at some time during the school year. Peer tutoring can also help reduce student achievement anxiety and fear of testing.

Within a school, peer tutoring, if properly introduced and maintained, can raise overall student classroom achievement. Peer tutoring is relatively easy for any classroom teacher to administer as a low-cost, supplemental teaching program. School administrators will often increase their support as the effects of tutoring in helping to improve standardized test scores become more apparent.

TWO EXAMPLES

In a local Chicago-area first-grade classroom, all the children were paired with other children from within their own classroom to tutor early reading skills. Students were paired so that there was a stronger and weaker reader in each pair. Each pair was then simultaneously trained in a tutoring training program carefully taught by the teacher.

Both students in the pair had an opportunity to be the tutor in each tutoring session, but the stronger student was the tutor first. The teacher assigned each pair to one of two class teams for which they earned points. The pairing and team assignments lasted four weeks.

During each peer tutoring session, the students earned points for successfully completing each first-grade reading activity. The students recorded the points they earned on their peer tutoring point sheet. The teacher also awarded bonus points during assessment observations if the tutor and tutee remained on task, cooperated with their partners, praised their partner, or the tutor gave specific compliments to the tutee. These bonus points helped reinforce both academic and social development.

At the end of every week, the teacher added up the points for each tutoring pair and announced the team totals. The winning team then stood up to take a bow while applauded by the second-place team. Then the winning team applauded the runner-up team, giving them public recognition for their good effort. Thus, the peer tutoring program gave the teacher a meaningful context to reinforce specific reading skills, while fostering a variety of social skills for each child.

In a cross-age peer tutoring program in New York City, high school students who were underachievers tutored elementary students in remedial reading. The high school tutors began to gradually assume the learning attitudes that their teacher trainers modeled.

The results were surprising. In just six months, the reading scores of the tutors rose by an equivalent of two years. In fact, the data show that the tutors generally benefited more than their tutees. Overlearning probably played a role in these results. Other similar case studies of older upper-grade students tutoring primary-grade children have yielded similar results in countless past research studies.

WHY USE PEER TUTORING?

There is extensive published research on the positive effects of peer tutoring. If so, why aren't peer tutoring classroom programs commonly used by teachers?

The biggest obstacle seems to be the belief that knowledge is best transferred when a child is taught by an adult. Other objections include:

- Too much time and effort to train tutors
- Tutor impatience
- Implications of tutor selection
- Academic subject suitability for peer tutoring
- Lack of expertise on the tutors part

As we see later, easy-to-use, proven peer tutoring methods have been developed that positively address all of these teacher concerns.

There also is broad general agreement that students will learn better when they help teach one another than they will in completely teacher-directed classrooms. The most commonly cited benefits of peer tutoring accrue to both tutor and tutee:

- The learning of academic skills
- Encouraging more positive attitudes toward learning
- Gaining a deeper understanding of subject areas
- Developing a more positive self-image
- Improving attitudes toward school and teachers

Teachers often find that an important by-product of peer tutoring is a more pleasant classroom atmosphere. Another potential benefit is better-adjusted students with skills transferable to parenting when they mature.

As students are trained in preparation to become tutors, their motivation to learn increases, personal feelings of helplessness are reduced, and the stigma fades of accepting help from others. Since all students have the chance to participate and the opportunity to help, peer tutoring empowers them to feel valuable and worthwhile. From these roots grows a more cooperative classroom learning spirit.

A wide range of specific K-12 subjects or special student populations can benefit from peer tutoring. Subjects include language arts, math, science, social studies, health, art, and other secondary school academic topics. Research has also shown that a broad range of regular and special-needs students, including low achievers, the socially disadvantaged, the learning disabled, the severely disabled, the mentally handicapped, and children with language delays, autism, or attention deficit disorder/hyperactivity disorders, can receive academic benefits from peer tutoring.

Student tutors experience improved personal locus of control, self-esteem, and social skills. They may also show a more positive attitude toward school and lower dropout rates, truancy, and tardiness.

Students profit from both traditional instruction and peer tutoring. However, research shows that when combined, school achievement may increase, race relations improve, and student socialization may become higher.

Teachers today are pressed for time. With a minimum time investment in peer tutoring, teachers can act as more powerful role models. They can transfer positive learning behaviors into the classroom and positive social behaviors that can be used at home, such as helping brothers and sister with homework. This promise of peer tutoring, particularly for disadvantaged or special-needs students, cannot be ignored by teachers who can more powerfully integrate learning both inside and outside the school.

ADDING PEER TUTORING TO YOUR TEACHING REPERTOIRE

This book has been prepared with the idea that only the fundamental concepts of peer tutoring—the who, what, why, when, and how—will be of real value to classroom teachers.

Every teacher knows the advantage of having certain learning tasks performed by a whole group of students at the same time. But every teacher also knows the frustration of too many students showing they don't understand the things that you just taught.

Any teacher who can daily keep the majority of his students at a high level of interest in learning something new is a teacher with the greatest skill. Unfortunately, in every classroom there is always a great deal of material to learn that, for many students, is potentially dull and unexciting.

Peer tutoring can be useful in helping students see added aspects of this material that prompts new questions. Peer tutoring increases students' motivation by enlisting their personal interest with success in mastering something and thereby gaining the "rank" of tutor.

This simple reward system appeals to the student's interest in receiving public recognition in a positive way. Peer tutoring is a novel way of teaching since it piques the student's interest to imitate the teacher. In the classroom, imitation plays an absolutely vital role, "Come and let me show you how."

Once it stimulates the student's motivation, peer tutoring frequently generates a curiosity to learn the next steps to be mastered in a subject, so that the student can then be a tutor himself or herself. This is based on a simple learning concept taken from the psychologist William James when he wrote long ago, "The child always attends more to what a teacher does, than what the same teacher says" (1901, p. 92).

2

DEFINING AND PLANNING
A PEER TUTORING PROGRAM

Five steps are essential for a teacher to plan and execute a successful peer tutoring program:

1. Selecting the tutoring partners and program goals
2. Designing the tutoring curriculum
3. Tutor training (A comprehensive tutor-training program is presented in chapter 3.)
4. Monitoring the program
5. Evaluation

Your effective short-term and long-term planning before the peer tutoring program begins will largely determine the degree to which student learning will actually increase. Proper planning will save you time and later frustration. It will also be easier to spot problems earlier and make adjustments more quickly to different elements of the peer tutoring program.

SELECTING PARTNERS AND GOALS

The first obvious task is: How are you going to select the tutors and tutees? Your selection will be largely driven by the goals of the peer-tutoring program. Whose performance are you going to improve: the tutor's, the tutee's, or both?

Scenario #1
Low performers are the tutees. High performers are the tutors.
This tutoring program is designed mainly to benefit the tutee. Teachers will usually select tutors who have already mastered the academic subject material and who need little additional training in the skill area to be tutored.

Scenario #2
Both tutor and tutee are deficient in required academic or social skills. Teachers will need to allot additional training time for creating a partnership with the tutors. The training activities are intended to foster the development of the social/academic skills on the part of the tutors. The tutors then reinforce these skills with the tutees.

Scenario #3

Low achieving students improve their own skills when given the responsibility of tutoring younger children. There is conflicting evidence on the relative differences between tutor and tutee. Teachers logically select their highest achieving students as tutors, though teachers might consider giving more weight to the personality characteristics of potential tutors, rather than their academic or intellectual credentials. It is often well advised to select tutors who will grow through the tutorial experience.

Certainly, tutors will increase their academic skills through the tutoring program. However, of equal importance for the tutor will be the personal growth of a relationship with another student. Tutoring will encourage the acquisition of important interpersonal and metacognitive skills.

DESIGNING THE TUTORING PROGRAM

Peer tutoring requires a basic program curriculum that preestablishes a sequence of learning objectives and a system for tutors to measure the tutee's mastery of each objective.

A tutor is not a professional teacher, but is used more as a learning technician. Tutoring activities need to be specified in detail through specific instruction for the tutor. Let's consider three different types of peer tutoring programs:

1. Content Programs (Subject Analysis)
   A subject analysis that specifies what is to be taught.
2. Lesson Programs (Prescriptive Diagnosis)
   A diagnostic-prescriptive approach that uses feedback from the tutee's response to the tutoring lesson. An additional remedial loop or bypass program of the skills that have been mastered follows in the next lesson.
3. Item Programs (Teaching Treatment)
   Face-to-face procedures for teaching whatever is specified by the lesson programs.

Why do some students fail to learn certain complex tasks in the classroom? Often they have not mastered certain skills required by that task. If these prerequisite skills have not been learned, teachers need to give the student immediate feedback. Peer tutoring can relieve some of this excessive feedback load upon the teacher by delegating parts of the instructional activities to the student peer tutors.

Immediate feedback is provided to the tutee for learning. The tutor receives feedback to know what to do next (short-term diagnosis) and for long-term diagnosis. The effectiveness of this feedback is clearly a function of the care with which the procedures are developed for a specific peer-tutoring program.

These important feedback procedures include:

1. Small, carefully sequenced steps in context
2. Use of positive reinforcement
3. Explicitly defined behavioral objectives
4. Careful planning and use of learning activities
5. Immediate knowledge of results
6. Continuous and explicit responding activity
7. Tutor self-sufficiency in providing desired behavioral outcomes
8. Active learning
9. Discovery learning
10. Individualized instruction

Teachers need to give the tutors clear, measurable learning objectives at the beginning of each tutoring session. This gives the tutor a clear description of what the learner will be able to do after the instruction. Without clear objectives, the teacher will find it impossible to measure reliably what the tutor-tutee were able to accomplish.

Tutors must be provided with materials for teaching the identified skills and reaching the learning objectives. Also, tutoring procedures must be carefully taught and role-played.

MONITORING THE PROGRAM

Your peer tutoring program will need a simple system for tutors to record data on each lesson. This helps make the tutor accountable to the teacher. This monitoring system allows the teacher to adjust the tutoring on a day-to-day basis. A good peer tutoring administrative record system includes:

1. The tutoring session's learning objectives
2. The tutoring procedures/methods used
3. Comments by the tutor on progress or mastery in reaching the objectives

Some of the pertinent basic management system questions you need to consider include:

1. What kinds of tutoring data will be kept?
2. How will the teacher monitor progress?
3. How often?
4. How will the teacher make decisions on program content changes, additions, altering tutor-tutee pairing?

Before the peer program begins, it is essential for teachers to contact parents and secure their written permission for their children to participate as tutors or tutees. (See Figures 2.1 and 2.2.) Establish a firm deadline

---

October 1, 20_____

Dear Mr. and Mrs. _____ :

To increase student learning, we are offering a classroom peer tutoring program. _____ has been selected to participate in our program as tutor for another student _____ (student name). The daily tutoring sessions would last _____ (time allotted) so that our program would not be a substitute for_____ (name) regular math program.

If you agree that _____ should be a part of our program, please sign the attached permission slip and return it to school by ____(specify date)____ .

If you have any questions, please feel free to call one of us at _____(school name)_____ (000) 000-0000 any morning but Friday, or e-mail me at _____(e-mail address)_____ .

Sincerely,

Teacher
_____

I give permission for _____ to participate in a peer tutoring program.

_____
Signature

_____
Date

Figure 2.1.   Sample Permission Form for Tutors

October 1, 20____

Dear Mr. and Mrs. _____ :

Our school provides peer tutoring to help students further improve their classroom learning.

_____ has been selected to participate in our peer tutoring program in order that he or she may obtain additional help in (example of program)____ skills.

OR

_____ has expressed a strong desire to participate in this program so that he or she may learn _____ (example of program)_____ .

If you agree that _____ should be a part of our program, please sign the attached permission slip and return it to school by _____ .

If you have any questions, please feel free to call one of us at _____(school name)_____ (000) 000-0000 any morning but Friday, or e-mail me at _____(e-mail address)_____ .

Sincerely,

Teacher

_____

I give permission for _____ to participate in a peer tutoring program.

_____
Signature

_____
Date

Figure 2.2. Sample Permission Form for Tutees

for the permission forms to be returned by the parents. A simple fact sheet that outlines your peer tutoring program should accompany the request for permission. You can also list the many learning advantages for both the tutor and the tutee such as the following:

1. A positive change in student attitudes toward school, themselves, other students, and learning in general.
2. Students retain many academic skills after the tutoring ends.
3. Parents of the tutees saw them more interested in reading and math (or subject tutored), reading more at home, and reading independently.
4. Parents of peer tutors also saw growth in academic and social skills and greater self-confidence.
5. Tutors improved their academic skills as a result of "overlearning" (i.e., teaching and reviewing basic skills).

After the tutors have been trained and the program begins, the teacher needs to decide how often to monitor the tutors through observations, conduct tutor retraining classes, and offer additional motivational incentives to both the tutor and tutee. Chapter 4 provides more details on how to best monitor daily results.

EVALUATION

Teachers need to match specific students' skills with potential tutoring activities. A simple prescriptive pretest at the beginning of the school year, or given in subtests periodically throughout the year, is one option to establish a student skill baseline. Another alternative is a criterion-referenced test that is based on the content of the school's curriculum objectives.

From a pretest, a plan can be written containing the learning objectives that the students need to master. Simple posttesting can be done throughout the year, sometimes by the tutor, to determine when skills have reached mastery.

Perhaps the most valuable feedback on the tutoring program will come from the students themselves. They can often give the most reliable information on such crucial issues as:

1. How many of the instructional objectives were mastered by the tutee?
2. What learning program changes were made based on the tutee's progress toward these objectives?
3. What learning goals did the tutor achieve with the tutee?
4. How well did the peer tutoring program promote a lively learning atmosphere in the classroom?

Measurement of results is an important part of any peer tutoring program for several significant reasons. As a motivator, students, parents, and teachers will respond in giving more collaborative support, if they have a feeling that real progress toward student learning is happening on a daily basis. Another compelling need for measurement is that everyone has the right to know how well they are doing in mastering specific skills.

Often the results of tutoring can be measured in terms of performance on a particular task relative to some standard set for that task (e.g., John can identify 90 percent of the U.S. state capitals). Many school districts use criterion-referenced tests for the local curriculum being taught. These tests can be used to establish peer tutoring instruction to a specific objective. We will have additional suggestions for assessing peer tutoring results in chapter 5.

Let us now turn to the most important single component in any peer tutoring program—tutor training.

TRAINING PEER TUTORS:
"PEOPLE LEARN WHILE THEY TEACH"

WHY TRAIN?

This chapter reviews the basic principles and procedures for an effective training program for student peer tutors. We will also consider different peer tutoring models. The next chapter follows up by giving detailed case-study applications of peer tutor training programs.

An important underlying principle to make any peer tutoring program effective is K.I.S.S.—"Keep It Simple for Students." You will be training students, not teachers. Too complex training, record keeping, or administration will only be self-defeating. Students will quickly lose interest. You will be further buried in unwarranted paperwork.

At the other extreme are teachers who frequently assume that just bringing together two students, and calling one a tutor, will automatically produce good results. Wrong, and here's why.

Two groups, trained and untrained peer tutors, were assigned to tutor math in a third-grade classroom. Both groups used the same teaching materials and spent the same amount of time tutoring. Teachers observing these tutoring session discovered that the trained tutors closely followed specific tutoring procedures and used positive reinforcement with the tutees. On the other hand, the untrained tutors constantly interfered with the tutees learning efforts. They punished, overcued repeatedly, and failed to give verbal praise or provide needed feedback before the tutee made the appropriate response.

Peer tutoring will be successful when:

1. The tutee is paired with a student tutor whose role is highly structured.
2. The tutor knows how to apply basic principles of learning.
3. The tutor comprehends how to use tutoring materials appropriate to the goals of the learning program.

PRETRAINING ISSUES

A typical peer tutoring training program flowchart is outlined in Figure 3.1. The flowchart shows the principal events of a typical training program. (Please refer back to Figure 3.1 as we review different tutor-training models.)

It is important to note that tutors are usually selected from students who have already learned the material. Also, both tutors and tutees need to know about the peer tutoring program before any training begins.

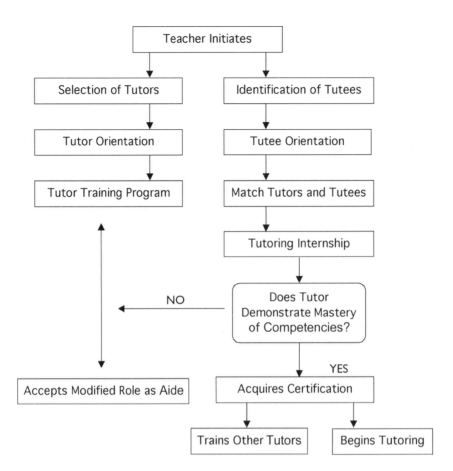

Figure 3.1. Flowchart of the Peer Tutor Training Program

Students need to understand:

1. The role of the teacher as a resource, consultant, and monitor.
2. Tutoring will not replace your classroom teaching.
3. Everyone will be given an opportunity to become a tutor based on their classroom work.

At the beginning of your tutor train-the-trainer program, you will need to make decisions on the following issues:

1. How many training sessions will be given to the tutors?
2. What will you cover in each session?
3. What will be the length of each student tutoring session?
4. How will you motivate the tutors during the tutoring program?
5. How will the tutors be monitored?

TRAINING-LEARNING PROGRAM MODELS

Training programs for tutors teach students basic learning principles that they will use to tutor, motivate, and assess results. Students learn to recognize the learning styles of a tutee and their own tutoring style. They learn the rudiments of what they are going to tutor (content) and the best ways how to tutor it (methods).

An effective tutor training program features a precise format of activities that control the entire process from the beginning to the end of each tutoring session. Training must allow the tutor time to practice the desired behavior and procedures and not just talk about it! Let's review several different alternative checklists that will help you design an effective tutor training program. Each training model is different from the others. Feel free to blend elements from each in preparing the training program that will be most effective for your specific student population.

Alternative #1

- Promoting a Tutoring Environment
  - _____ 1. Establish a rapport with the tutee (one minute).
  - _____ 2. Express empathy.
  - _____ 3. Ask questions about interests.
  - _____ 4. Talk about common interests.
  - _____ 5. Be candid and frank.
  - _____ 6. Spend five minutes of the first class establishing the "tone" for meetings.
  - _____ 7. Acknowledge tutee's positive or negative response to tutoring activities.
  - _____ 8. Get the tutee's attention.
  - _____ 9. Give clear instructions. Let the tutee know precisely how to respond.
  - ___ 10. Sit next to the tutee, not across from him or her or at an angle.
  - ___ 11. Give extensive positive feedback immediately and often!
  - ___ 12. Don't say "no," or "that is wrong." Instead, give the correct answer and how you got it.
  - ___ 13. Repeat the answer with the tutee.
  - ___ 14. Have the tutee say the answer alone.
  - ___ 15. If the tutee is struggling, give the correct answer.
  - ___ 16. Avoid punishing the tutee.
  - ___ 17. Give special recognition for achievement.
  - ___ 18. Tell someone (the teacher or another student) about success.
  - ___ 19. Give special privileges.
  - ___ 20. Give a reward for completing a difficult task.
  - ___ 21. Always clarify expectations—what specifically do you want the tutee to do.
- The Tutoring Plan
  - _____ 1. Pretest and diagnose learning issues.
  - _____ 2. Select skills to be tutored.
  - _____ 3. Establish realistic goals both short term (class) and long term (semester).
  - _____ 4. Clarify goals and return to them often.
  - _____ 5. Measure daily progress in reaching them.
  - _____ 6. Establish your rules and regulations at the first tutoring class.
  - _____ 7. Select and organize appropriate learning materials.
  - _____ 8. Keep a Tutor Diary as an outline of each class. (See Figure 3.2.)
  - _____ 9. Issue a Tutoring Class Report to the tutee and his or her parents. (See Figure 3.3.)
  - ___ 10. Test developmentally with short exercises or quizzes.
- Learning Habits
  - _____ 1. Carefully develop the drill and practice materials to be used.
  - _____ 2. Personal success brings acceptance of repetition.
  - _____ 3. Memory of a learned skill may fade.
  - _____ 4. Overlearning (repetition) is sometimes helpful.
  - _____ 5. Student attention span is usually thirty to sixty minutes.
  - _____ 6. A tutee must completely master a skill before the tutor introduces a new skill.
  - _____ 7. Each mastered skill is recorded.

Tutor: _____ School: _____ Grade: _____

Teacher: _____ Student: _____

Date	Time Period	Tutoring Activity	Results	

Figure 3.2. Example of Tutor Diary

Tutee Progress Report

Tutee _____ Grade _____

Age _____ School _____

Room No. _____ Teacher _____

Tutoring Class Session Date _____

Skills Mastered:

_____

_____

_____

Tutor _____

Figure 3.3.   Example of Tutoring Class Report

How to Be a Good Tutor:

1. Be on time.
2. Start the class with a nice question.
3. Be kind and cheerful.
4. Use time wisely.
5. Always plan and be ready for the class.
6. Always be pleasant to the tutee; never scold.
7. Use simple directions
8. Keep your Tutor Diary and records clear, accurate, and up to date.
9. Offer praise, for example, "Super," "Excellent," or "Cool."
10. Have different ways of rewarding the tutee.
11. Avoid saying: "You're Wrong," "Incorrect," "No."
12. Don't make the tutee feel stupid or inferior.
13. Highlight the tutee's progress so that tutoring is fun.
14. Remember "KISS:" "Keep it simple for students."
15. Enjoy being a tutor.

Figure 3.4.   A Job Aid for Tutors

Alternative #2—Stimulus-Response Program

- ____ Step 1. Preassess the student's present ability.
  1. Select appropriate instructional outcomes.
  2. Prepare a record of the student's progress (Tutor Diary).
  3. Prepare a pretest.
  4. Pretest the student.
  5. Record the student's performance in the Tutor Diary.
- ____ Step 2. Prepare to tutor the student.
  1. Prepare instructional materials, for example, flash cards.
  2. Prepare a record of daily tutoring activities (Tutor Diary).
  3. Specify instructional strategies.
- ____ Step 3. Tutor the student using the proper tutoring techniques and procedures. (See Figure 3.4.)
  1. Follow general tutoring techniques and procedures.
  2. Follow specific tutoring techniques and procedures.
- ____ Step 4. Maintain the appropriate records (Tutor Diary).
- ____ Step 5. Review the student's progress.
  1. Systematically review instructional prescriptions previously learned.
  2. Administer the delayed posttest.

See examples of stimulus-response outcomes for preschool (Figure 3.5) and the primary grades (Figure 3.6).

Preschool Level

The child will name the lower/uppercase letters of the alphabet without hesitation and when they are presented out of order.

The child will name the digits 1–20 without hesitation and when they are presented out of order.

The child will name basic geometric shapes (e.g., ○, △, □, etc) without hesitation.

The child will name the eight basic colors (red, yellow, blue, orange, green, purple, white, black) without hesitation.

The child will name without hesitation common objects or animals that were previously unknown by the child (e.g., orange, tiger, etc.).

Figure 3.5.   Example of Stimulus-Response Instructional Outcomes—Preschool
Source: Harrison & Guymon (1980).

Primary Grade Levels

The child will produce the sounds of the consonants without hesitation.

The child will produce the short sound of all five vowels without hesitation.

The child will produce the sounds of the common digraphs and blends without hesitation (e.g., th, sh, wh, fl, bl, pr, etc.).

The child will read 200 basic sight words without hesitation (e.g., the, they, said, so for, because, etc.).

The child will name designated historical characters without hesitation when presented with their pictures (e.g., George Washington, Benjamin Franklin, Abraham Lincoln, etc.).

The child will orally provide synonyms for 500 basic words without hesitation (e.g., glad, funny, pretty, bad, hot, etc.).

The child will name the digits 20–100 without hesitation when they are presented out of order.

The child will read three-digit numbers without hesitation (e.g., 137, 546, 389, etc.).

The child will say the time of day without hesitation when presented with pictures of clocks either at the hour or half past the hours.

The child will say without hesitation the names of the months of the year when presented with abbreviations of the names.

The child will name the basic signs without hesitation (e.g., $+$, $-$, $\times$, %, $, etc.).

Figure 3.6. Example of Stimulus-Response Instructional Outcomes—Primary Grades
Source: Harrison & Guymon (1980).

Alternative #3—Sample Steps for a Tutoring Program

_____ 1. Put a skill outcome in writing before each class based on present tutee knowledge, classroom learning needs, and personal area of interest.

_____ 2. Record results of pretest.

_____ 3. Initiate a vocabulary activity.

_____ 4. Have tutee read aloud.

_____ 5. Give tutee a passage to read silently.

_____ 6. Focus on finding the main idea of the passage.

_____ 7. Review session's work.

_____ 8. Administer posttest

_____ 9. Keep a daily diary of tutorial work.

_____ 9. Praise tutee for daily accomplishments.

_____ 10. Give a Daily Progress Report for tutee's parents. Explain what this is.

Alternative #4—Cross-Age Tutoring Program

The following tutor training program was designed for an elementary school cross-age tutoring program using fifth-graders to tutor kindergarten students.

- Orientation Training and Supervision of Independent Activities
  1. Fifth-graders (first group):
     Step 1. Selected by own teacher—four per class. (Criteria: Initial tutors should be leader types.)
     Step 2. Receive introduction to tutoring from tutor-trainer: three to five days, thirty minutes per day.
        a. Purposes, types of tutoring
        b. General procedures for working with a learner
        c. Role-playing with tutor-trainer
        d. Role-playing with each other
     Step 3. Kindergarten teacher informs class about tutors and the role of tutors.
     Step 4. Kindergarten teacher introduces tutors to class.
     Step 5. Tutors supervise independent learning activities of tutees for one to two weeks to become familiar with the children.
     Step 6. Kindergarten teacher meets with tutors:
        a. On first tutoring day, to explain supervision of independent activities
        b. Weekly, to review past week's work and to plan for the next week's work
        c. Weekly, for tutors and teachers to discuss performance and problems
        d. On the spot, to train tutors on specific activities and procedures
     Step 7. Additional training by tutor-trainer when necessary.
  2. Fifth-graders (second group of tutors):
     Step 1 and Step 2: Same as for first group.
     Step 3. Kindergarten teacher introduces tutors to class, only after first group is functioning smoothly.
     Step 4. Kindergarten teacher meets with tutors—first day, weekly, on the spot.
     Step 5. Tutors supervise independent activities—two weeks.
  3. Evaluation of tutors: By tutor-trainer at end of training, and by teacher, during supervision of independent activities. Use a standard rating form.
- Tutoring for Specific Instructional Objectives (Kindergarten teachers see and react to materials and procedures prior to implementation.)

1. Fifth-graders (first group are inexperienced tutors):

    Step 1. Receive training on specific objectives from tutor-trainer—one week.

    a. Purpose, materials, procedures

    b. Demonstration by tutor-trainer

    c. Role-playing with trainer

    d. Role-playing with each other

    Step 2. Tutors observe demonstration by Kindergarten teacher in front of the whole class, or part of the class, as appropriate. Tutors complete classroom observation forms (Figure 3.7).

    Step 3. Practice tutoring with Kindergarten learners—one week.

    a. One tutor, one to two learners

    b. Kindergarten teacher observes practice tutoring

    Step 4. Kindergarten teacher meets with tutors.

    a. At the end of practice tutoring to make recommendations

    b. On the spot to deal with specific problems

    c. During weekly conferences.

2. Experienced tutors with new objectives and materials: (1) Similar to prior objectives (demonstration by Kindergarten teacher in front of whole class; tutors receive materials for review on own). (2) Different from prior objectives—tutors receive training from tutor-trainer as necessary.

3. Fifth-graders (second group):

    Step 1. Receive training on specific objectives—one week.

    a. One at time are released from supervision of independent activities

    b. Trained by tutor-trainer

    c. Later, fifth-graders trained by experienced tutors

    Step 2. Practice tutoring under supervision of experienced tutor and Kindergarten teacher—one week.

4. Evaluation of tutors

- Ongoing Tutoring

    1. Types of tutoring:

    a. Supervision of independent activities

    b. Tutoring for specific objectives

    c. Tutors alternate between the two types

    2. Assignment of individual learners to tutors:

    a. Each tutor is assigned three to four learners from one class

    b. Kindergarten teacher and tutor-trainer make assignments based on strengths and weaknesses of tutors that were observed during training, and based on Kindergarten teacher's knowledge of Kindergarten learners

    3. Testing of learners:

    a. Tutor pretests every learner for each specific objective before beginning tutoring for that objective

    b. Tutor tests each learner for mastery of an objective whenever the tutor feels the learner is ready

    c. When necessary, an especially designated tutor will administer mastery tests, to take load off a tutor

    4. Record keeping:

    a. At first, records are kept by Kindergarten teacher, so that tutors do not become overloaded

    b. When tutors have experience and are comfortable with tutoring, the tutors and learners will keep their own record of progress on prepared forms

- Suggested Activities in Fifth-Grade Sending Class

    1. Teacher and tutors meet for a weekly conference.

    2. Tutors share experience with class. Teacher and tutors discuss problems with class and solicit class suggestions.

Classroom Observation Report

Name: _____

1. Write down two rules in effect in the classroom you visited.

2. What did the teacher do/say to establish a relationship/show mutual trust with his or her students?

3. Write examples of ways the teacher praised the students for appropriate work/behavior.

4. How did the teacher correct incorrect responses?

5. What was the teacher doing during the times when students worked independently?

6. Did any students do something other than follow the directions the teacher gave? What?

7. Write examples of ways the teacher indicated disapproval of inappropriate behavior?

8. Write three things you liked about the class.

9. Write three things didn't like about the class.

10. Write two specific things you saw the teacher do.

11. Write two specific things you saw the students do.

Figure 3.7. Classroom Observation by Student for Cross-Age Tutor Training

3. Tutors bring Kindergarten children to fifth-grade class to meet older students and tell what they do together.
4. Tutors post pictures of Kindergarten students in class.
5. Sending teacher integrates tutoring with English by relating writing assignments to tutoring (e.g., tutors may keep daily diary—highlights, not detailed).
6. Sending teacher exchanges class for an hour with Kindergarten teacher. Kindergarten teacher explains Kindergarten program, schedule, and materials; tells what Kindergarten children are like and what goals of Kindergarten year are; and solicits and answers questions.
7. Half of fifth and one-half of Kindergarten class exchange students for one-to-one tutoring.

- Training Schedule (All Tutors are Fifth-Graders)

Week 1. (1) Group I tutors selected. (2) Group I tutors receive orientation training.

Week 2. (1) Group I tutors supervise independent activities. (2) Group II tutors selected. (3) Group II tutors receive orientation training.

Week 3. (1) Group I tutors receive training on specific objectives. (2) Group II tutors supervise independent activities.

Week 4. (1) Group I tutors tutor for specific objectives. (2) Group II tutors supervise independent activities.

Week 5. (1) Group I tutors supervise independent activities. (2) Group II tutors receive training on specific objectives.

Week 6. (1) Group I tutors supervise independent activities. (2) Group II tutors tutor for specific objectives.

Week 7. (1) Tutoring and supervision ongoing with eight tutors for each Kindergarten class. Each tutor assigned to three to four Kindergarten learners.

HOW MANY TRAINING SESSIONS?

Tutor training must last as long as it takes for students to master these essential skills. A time-efficient way to accomplish this end is to use role-playing sessions as the final part of the training.

Step 1. The trainer models the tutoring procedure while the tutor-trainee plays the part of the learner.
Step 2. The roles are now reversed. The trainer becomes the tutee and the tutor practices the required tutoring skills.

A useful way to reinforce the training is to immediately increase the tutor's visibility in the "teacher" role. Give the tutor a portfolio to carry containing the daily tutor diary, lesson outcomes, daily progress report, checklist for learning, checklist for skill acquisition, and so on. Students need concrete examples to reinforce your training. Many enjoy just having record-keeping paraphernalia.

At the last training class, consider having each tutor present her or his plan for the first tutoring session. What are the goals? What tutoring materials will he or she use? What form is the pretest/posttest? Role-play the session with the student.

It can be very useful to ask the tutor to list three events (on cards) he or she expects to happen during the first session. Use these cards for discussion. Save this information for posttraining. It will be helpful for students to compare their expectations with what really happened.

Award certificates after they have completed the tutoring training program. At the end of the school year, distribute more elaborate Master Tutor Diplomas for those student tutors who have continued with the program through the school year. Parental feedback has shown that many tutors are very proud of these awards and display them at home. Teachers might consider rewarding these tutors with a party at the end of the year.

TUTORING TIME AND SPACE CONSIDERATIONS

To anchor training efforts, the teacher will need to decide when, where, and how long in length each tutoring session will be. Also the teacher must plan when to begin the peer tutoring program and when to end the program.

Most teachers have found that a minimum of three tutoring sessions per week, of sixty minutes per session, is most effective to achieve increased student performance. They also can be held on a daily basis. Much will be determined by the attention span of the tutor and tutee. Older students benefit from longer tutoring sessions; younger children from a shorter one. Your main focus should be that both students have a successful learning experience.

Tutoring sessions can be scheduled during regular class time, before school, during lunch hour, or after school. Whenever they are held, of whatever length, it is vitally important for the teacher to establish a specific tutoring session schedule and abide by it. Students need to experience order and have a system to plan their own tutoring activity.

Scheduling a cross-age peer tutoring session requires the two collaborating teachers (one teacher sending the tutors to the second teacher of the tutees) to coordinate their class schedules.

You may also consider establishing a tutoring quarter or "tutoring semester" system based on report cards, testing, or other regular school year calendar events. This will give both the tutor and tutee a specific time period to work toward achieving the learning goals they establish as part of the program.

Where will the peer tutoring session be held? Possible sites may include a quiet corner of your classroom or other unoccupied areas in the school building (such as the cafeteria, the auditorium, the library, the computer learning center) either during or after regular school hours. In some programs, peer tutoring was done in a student's home after school or on the weekend, and other sessions were held at school. Weather and climate permitting, tutoring might be done out of doors.

HIGH SCHOOL PEER TUTORING

Secondary-level peer tutor training is different from the other training models in several respects.

- Training Program
  1. Three-Session Format

     1st Class—Teacher demonstrates the tutoring procedures. Tutors follow with a step-by-step written outline.

     2nd Class—Several tutors implement the process with other students acting as tutees.

     3rd Class—Remaining tutors are trained by others who have role-played during the second session.
  2. Formal training is kept to a minimum because the training is more generic and does not apply to any single subject-content area.
  3. What are the management competencies to be achieved by the end of the tutor train-the-trainer program?
     a. How to state and implement the steps of tutoring program
     b. How to keep and interpret records
     c. Tutors know their limits and how to refer to a teacher
  4. What are the instructional competencies to be achieved by the end of the conclusion of the tutor training program?
     a. Mastery of skill content
     b. Ability to write tutoring objectives
     c. Identification of task-related subskills
     d. Diagnosis of tutee's learning weaknesses and how to tutor to them
     e. Identification of tutee's learning strengths and how to build on them to overcome weaknesses and increase motivation

    f. Organization of tutoring session learning activities

    g. Varying the tutoring content and style from session to session

    h. The use of good questioning skills with the tutee

- Tutor Use of Learning Materials
  1. Properly organizes learning materials for each tutoring session.
  2. Makes good use of these materials with the tutee.
  3. Administers and interprets tests and quizzes.
- Interpersonal Skills
  1. Tutor uses positive reinforcement with the tutee.
  2. Tutor learns how to personally motivate the tutee's achievement.
  3. Tutor assumes the role of a leader.
  4. Tutor is able to develop a positive rapport with the tutee.
- Peer Tutoring Session in Five Steps

  1st Step—Review session material.

  2nd Step—Set session objectives.

  3rd Step—Present session material.

  4th Step—Evaluate session.

  5th Step—Arrange next class (homework).

PEER TUTORING CHALLENGES

Parents are often concerned that peer tutors will be absent from their class and will fall behind in their own work. Research has shown that this seldom happens even when a student is tutoring every day. Instead, the opposite occurs. Peer tutors usually develop higher levels of both motivation and stronger subject content from their own learning as well as that of the tutees.

Motivating students to learn how to learn, to internalize the need to learn and are major reasons that teachers support peer tutoring. A focus on these so-called metacognitive, higher level thinking skill activities remains one of the chief challenges of contemporary classroom teaching. The many positive motivational and instructional aspects of peer tutoring reinforce individual critical-thinking skills. Peer tutoring often helps the teacher address the reasons that many K-12 students give for their disinterest in academic achievement. These include:

- Students are preoccupied with peer-status concerns.
- It isn't "cool" to be interested in academic work. Peer leaders are antilearning; or the group norm is antilearning.
- Students see themselves as dumb and inadequate.
- Students see little or no relevance of their studies to real life.
- Adolescents have strong antiadult and antiteacher attitudes. Students want "freedom" from teachers and adults.
- Adolescents have strong antischool work attitudes.
- No one gives students individualized attention. The teacher never has time. He or she is always "too busy."
- Classroom instruction has no way to help someone who does not understand without publicly admitting to personal ignorance. This is too embarrassing in front of your peer group.
- Classwork does not challenge some students' ability. It is too simple, repetitive and boring.

We now have outlined the most important facets of organizing a peer tutoring training program. In the next chapter, we review specific training program examples of peer tutoring applications for different age groups, special needs, and subject areas.

4

TRAINING PROGRAM CASE STUDIES: "TO TEACH IS TO LEARN TWICE"

Just suggesting a classroom peer tutoring program to teachers causes many of them to "head for the hills" and hide out. Most teachers will say that their work schedules are already too full, with no classroom time left for peer tutoring. However, after they see the great enthusiasm of many student tutors and tutees, most teachers begin to see the value of peer tutoring methods.

As they begin to experience increased student achievement, both teachers and administrators rearrange time and space priorities to incorporate peer tutoring into daily classroom and school operations.

TUTORING CASE STUDIES

Let's review several real-world peer tutoring case studies for students at different academic levels and having a variety of educational needs.

Training Case Study # 1—Third-Grade Classroom

Setting:	Math Peer Tutoring Twenty-Minute Sessions Monday through Thursday
Rationale for Tutoring:	Students observed by teacher or aide as experiencing difficulty learning the basic multiplication facts.
Pretesting:	Objective pretest and multiplication fact tests.
Permission:	Written parent permission requested for tutoring of tutee.
Choosing the Tutors:	Students who had earlier expressed a desire to work with others. Students who had stronger multiplication skills, but who could still profit from "over-learning" as a tutor. Written parental permission requested for students to become tutors.
Training Program:	Five 25-minute training sessions.
Session #1:	Teacher explains objectives of the program to students.

Materials are introduced.

Tutors are given the peer tutoring notebooks.

Responsibilities of a tutor are outlined.

Session #2:   Review of materials and procedures.

Tutors are introduced to Steps for Tutor to Use in a Session Sheet (see Figure 4.1). Class sessions are described in detail. Tutors are given Tutor Tips: Tutoring Session Management (see Figure 4.2). (You may wish to laminate these sheets to be kept at the front of the peer tutor notebooks.)

Teacher discusses the roles of the tutor and the tutee.

Teacher role-plays the tutoring session with a student.

Session #3:   The teacher and student tutor switch their roles and twice practice the tutoring procedures.

Session #4:   The tutees are introduced to the tutoring materials and procedures.

Students learn responsibilities as tutees.

Teacher role-plays the tutoring session with a tutee.

Session #5:   Tutor and tutee hold a tutoring session.

Before session begins:
   1. Look over flash cards for session.
   2. Fill out the Tutor Log (recording sheet) with student's name, date, and session number.
   3. Write the multiplication facts for the day on the recording sheet and the daily worksheet.
   4. If you have any questions, ask the teacher.
Begin session:
   1. Meet your partner and take him or her to the designated space. Smile and be friendly. Make your partner feel comfortable.
   2. Go over flash cards with answer side showing. Say "2 × 3 = 6" and have student repeat after you. Go through all ten flash cards.
   3. Give student a piece of scrap paper. Go through cards again with answer side showing. Say "2 × 3 = 6" and have student write the fact on the piece of paper. Go through all ten flash cards.
   4. Trial #1. Go through each flash card. Have student give answer. If answer is wrong, say "2 × 3 = 6" and have student repeat after you. Put card in separate pile and go on with rest of cards.
   5. Fill out recording sheet.
      + for right answers
      0 for wrong answers
   6. Give student fact quiz. Give her or him two minutes to complete. Use stopwatch.
   7. Correct quiz. Go over the quiz with student so that he or she knows the results.
   8. Mark the Tutor Log.
   9. Trial #2. If an answer is wrong, say "2 × 3 = 6" and have student repeat after you. Have him or her write "2 × 3 = 6." Say "2 × 3 = ?" Student says answer (+)
   10. Mark the Tutor Log.
   11. Check over Tutor Log: If student has received 3 +s on one problem, give cards to him or her to put on "learned word" ring.

   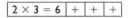

   12. Give student "feelings" card to fill out.
   13. Send student back into classroom.
   14. Set out new cards for the next session. Remember to include cards the student has received a 0 on and then take cards from new pile to make 10 new cards.
   15. Tutor fills out the bottom of the Tutor Log. Staple worksheet and recording sheet together. Put all materials away.
   16. Inform teacher that the session is over.

Figure 4.1.   Steps for Tutor to Use in a Session
Adapted from: Pierce, Stahlbrand, & Armstrong (1984).

How to Manage Your Tutoring Session

1. Always come prepared to tutor!
2. Maintain clear tutoring class rules and always use them.
3. Always be positive at the start of the tutoring session, give the tutee all your attention, and tell an interesting story. Go over class rules, the day's objectives, and recall a past class success.
4. Be sure to have the tutee's total attention before you start tutoring.
5. Signal the teacher if you need assistance.
6. Use positive reinforcement (praise) when the tutee is successful.
7. Provide feedback on each task the tutee completes.

IMPORTANT:
- Always overlook failure by the tutee in word or deed.
- Generously praise the tutee who is successful in following class assignments and completing them.

Figure 4.2. Tutor Tips: Tutoring Session Management

Teacher observes and offers suggestions and praise throughout the session.

The tutor is "certified" if the teacher believes that the tutoring pair will work together effectively. If not, either an additional training class can be held or the tutor paired with another student.

Peer Tutor's Notebook Materials:	Tutor Log (see Figure 4.3)
	Tutor Tips: Tutoring Session Management (Figure 4.2)
	Steps for Tutor to Use in a Session (Figure 4.1)
	A Job Aid for Tutors (How to Be a Good Tutor Sheet, see Figure 3.4)
	2 pencils
	Scrap paper
	Format for Daily Peer Quiz Sheet (see Figure 4.4)

Tutoring Session Procedures:

Step 1: At the appointed time, tutors get their tutoring notebooks and review flash cards for that day's session.

Step 2: Tutor fills out the preliminary information on Tutor Log and Format for Daily Peer Quiz Sheet (see Figures 4.3 and 4.4).

Step 3: Tutor takes tutee to tutoring work area.

Step 4: Flash card tutoring session procedure in five parts:

Components	Behavior
1. Say	Give a fact (2 x 3 = 6), the tutee will repeat after tutor.
2. Write	Given a fact (? x 3 = 6), the tutee will repeat after tutor and write fact on scrap paper.
3. Trial 1 answer	Given a fact (2 x 3 = ?), the tutee will give the answer.
4. Fact Quiz	Given 2 minutes, the tutee will write the answers to 10 fact problems.
5. Trial 2	Given a fact (2 x 3 = ?), the tutee will give the answer.

For parts #3, 4, and 5 the tutor scores the daily Tutor Log in the appropriate space. If the tutee is correct, the tutor gives praise and scores an A+ on the Tutor Log.

If tutee's answer is incorrect, a "0" is scored.

The following tutoring procedure is then used:

Tutor: 2 x 3 = ?
Tutee: 7
Tutor: 2 x 3 = 6
Tutee: 2 x 3 = 6
Tutor: Please write it
Tutee: (writes problem)
Tutor: 2 x 3 = ?
Tutee: 2 x 3 = 6

Tutor Log

Tutee: _____

Tutor: _____

Date: _____

Session Number: _____

Problem	Trial #1	Fact Quiz	Trial #2
1.			
2.			
3.			
4.			
5.			
6.			
7.			
8.			
9.			
10.			

What do you think about today's session? (Circle One)

1	2	3	4
Great	Good	Fair	Poor

Figure 4.3. Tutor Log (Case Study 1)
Adapted from: Pierce, Stahlbrand, & Armstrong (1984).

Quiz Report Sheet

Tutee: _____

Tutor: _____

Date: _____

Session Number: _____

X ____   X ____   X ____
X ____   X ____   X ____   X ____
X ____   X ____   X ____

Figure 4.4. Format for Daily Peer Quiz
Source: Pierce, Stahlbrand, & Armstrong (1984).

Step 5:   For the Daily Peer Quiz, the tutee is allowed to correct his or her Quiz Report Sheet (see Figure 4.4).

Step 6:   At the end of the tutoring session, the tutee is given the cards that he or she scored three pluses on. The student can keep these cards at school or take them home.

To ensure long-term retention by the tutee of these math facts, the teacher gives a thirty-five-problem fact test (oral or written) twice during the week (see Figure 4.5).

Step 7:   At the end of the tutoring session the tutee fills out a Feeling Card and goes back to his or her desk (see Figure 4.6).

The tutor fills out a similar rating scale at the bottom of the Tutor Log (Figure 4.3). All of that session's papers are then stapled together and placed in the peer tutoring notebook.

The tutor then takes out the next ten math flash cards to be tutored in the next session. The tutor then puts all the materials away in a designated storage area and reports back to the teacher that the session has been completed with the tutee.

RESULTS

From weekly test results the teacher believed that the math peer tutoring program was very successful. Both tutors and tutees increased their knowledge of multiplication facts as measured by the posttest. Generally, the students who participated also increased personal accuracy in their daily classroom math work.

Most students in a regular elementary school classroom can benefit from a simple skill-based peer tutoring program. With careful planning a set of skills in almost any subject area can be the program's learning objective. This instructional procedure takes a minimal amount of teacher time to prepare. Peer tutoring also allows the teacher to use more instructional time on complex topics rather than skill-set learning.

Training Case Study #2—Peer/Cross-Age Tutoring Program

Setting: Elementary School
             Special Education Math
             Twenty-Minute Session
             Three Sessions per Week
             Tutoring for Entire School Year

Rationale for Tutoring: *For tutees* who were elementary school students eligible for special education math services: 90 percent of students would achieve more than one month growth per month of tutoring as measured by curriculum objectives.

For tutors who are high school students: earn high school course credits in a challenging and enriching educational program.

Evaluation: Initial tutee prescriptions and class objectives are written for each tutor by the elementary and secondary teachers (see Figure 4.7).

Permission: Tutors sign a contract in the fall to:
             a. Attend all tutor-training classes
             b. Provide continuous service to their tutee for the entire school year.

Choosing the Tutors: In the spring, interested high school students were invited to a special slide/tape presentation on the peer tutoring program at their high school. Students then observed

Name: _____

Date: _____

Session Number: _____

Multiply:

X _____   X _____   X _____   X_____   X _____   X_____

X_____   X _____   X _____   X _____   X _____   X _____

X _____   X_____   X _____   X_____   X _____   X_____   X _____

X _____   X_____   X _____   X_____   X _____   X_____   X _____

X _____   X _____   X _____   X_____   X _____   X_____   X _____

                          X _____   X _____

Figure 4.5.   Format for Fact Test
Source: Pierce, Stahlbrand, & Armstrong (1984).

Name: _____

Date: _____

How was today's session?

(Circle One)　　　1. Great　　　2. Good　　　3. Fair　　　4. Poor

Comments: 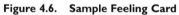_____

_____

_____

_____

Figure 4.6.　Sample Feeling Card

Setting Class Objectives

Class objectives must be observed behaviors. Objectives must be so concrete that anyone can see whether the tutee had or had not completed each objective.

Limit your objectives to behaviors or descriptions of what the tutee will do at the end of the tutoring session.

Objectives	Expected Final Behavior	Final Performance
1.		_ Accept _ Reject Describe:
2.		_ Accept _ Reject Describe:
3.		_ Accept _ Reject Describe:
4.		_ Accept _ Reject Describe:
5.		_ Accept _ Reject Describe:

Figure 4.7.   Setting Objectives

several cross-age tutoring sessions. If interested in the course, students completed an application form, including three references.

Training Program:	Cross-age tutoring sessions were based on school district curriculum objectives that included sequential instructional objectives, a monitoring system, an assessment system, and appropriate materials.
Tutoring Procedures Trained:	Attention getting Clear presentation Modeling Prompting and effective management techniques Setting and using curriculum objectives Recording attainment of objectives (see Figure 4.8) Tutors were tested on mastering these tutoring concepts Extensive class discussion
Monitoring:	Elementary teachers regularly monitor the progress of the tutor and tutee. Tutoring changes are made based on the rate of tutee skill acquisition. A Tutor Diary is kept by the tutor each day (see Figure 3.2). It is summarized monthly for the teachers.

RESULTS

The cross-age tutoring program revealed an average gain of 1.6 months of growth per one month of instruction. The high school tutors indicated that they had enjoyed the experience. The teacher trainers believed that the tutors gained higher level thinking skills. They saw the cross-age tutoring program as a useful metacognitive activity for their high school students.

Training Case Study #3—Peer/Cross-Age Tutoring in Primary Grades

Setting:	Elementary School Sight Word Recognition and Comprehension Tutoring Two-minute Sessions or Longer If Needed
Rationale for Tutoring:	Students had difficulty in letter and sound recognition skills.
Pretesting:	Three assessments were made of a student's oral word, letter name, and sound recognition skills on three separate testing days.
Choosing the Cross-Age Tutors:	Cross-age tutors from the upper or middle grades were selected who had mastered the complete sight vocabulary and who could follow exact directions.
Training Program:	Four training sessions
Session #1:	Trainer should tutor how to use the flash cards and scoring sheet. Including where to record date, data, and correct (+) or incorrect (0) responses by each word (see Figure 4.9). Trainer role-plays session. A reverse role-play is also done.

Math Curriculum Objective System

A. Basic Number Concepts   Prescription for: _____

The student will:	Pretest Mastery	Posttest Mastery
A-1 Count to ten orally		
A-2 Point to larger or smaller		
A-3 Point to shorter or longer		
A-4 Point to shorter or taller		
A-5 Point to lower or higher		
A-6 Point to fat or thin		
A-7 Mark the set that has more/less		
A-8 Count ordered set 0–10 objects orally		
A-9 Count unordered set 0–10 objects orally		
A-10 Name number when pointed to (0–10)		
A-11 Write dictated numbers 0–5		
A-12 Write dictated numbers 6–10		
A-13 Tell numbers that come after (0–10)		
A-14 Tell numbers that come before (0–10)		
A-15 Take given number of objects from set (1–10)		
A-16 Mark the sets that are equal		
A-17 Mark the set that has a smaller number		
A-18 Mark the set that has a larger number		
A-19 Match the set of objects with the number (0–10)		

Figure 4.8.   Sample Chart for Skills Mastery Sequences

Flash Card Scoring Sheet

Tutee: _____ Tutor: _____ Date: _____

Directions: Next to each word identified correctly put +, incorrectly put 0.

see	then	walk	yellow
seven	there	want	yes
shall	these	warm	you
she	they	was	your
show	think	wash	
sing	this	we	
sit	those	well	
six	three	went	
sleep	to	were	
small	today	what	
so	together	when	
some	too	where	
soon	try	which	
start	two	white	

Figure 4.9. Example of Flash Card Scoring Sheet

Session #2:   Review of information from first training session.

                       Tutor observes entire tutoring session with tutee. Cross-age tutor records session responses on practice scoring sheet.

                       After the session, the trainer and tutor privately discuss what occurred and compare their separate scoring sheets.

                       Trainer and tutor role-play and reverse roles part way through the session.

Session #3:   Review of tutoring procedures.

                       Role-play with trainer as tutee.

                       Cross-age tutor completes an entire session with student tutee. Trainer observes and assists if necessary.

Session #4:   Brief review and discussion of the finer points of being an effective tutor.

                       Tutor and tutee complete a session. The trainer observes.

Note: Training can be shortened as soon as tutor demonstrates mastery of tutoring objectives.

Tutoring Session
Procedures:

Step 1:   The tutor keeps all the tutoring materials in a folder in his or her classroom with the instructional materials to be used including flash cards, prepared scoring sheets, directions, and a pencil.

Step 2:   The tutor arrives as scheduled at the tutee's classroom and takes the student to the tutoring area. He or she takes out the materials to be used for the tutoring session and then dates the scoring sheet.

Step 3:   Using the scoring sheet, the tutor gives the first of three tests. The tutor shows the tutee a flash card. If the tutee waits more than five seconds to respond, gives an incorrect answer the first time, or gives no response at all, the tutors uses the following procedure:

                       a. The tutor says, "The word (phrase or number) is _____."
                       b. The tutee repeats _____.
                       c. The tutor says, "Look at the word carefully and say it again."
                       d. Tutee repeats the word.
                       e. Tutor marks the scoring sheet next to the word with a "0."
                       f. Tutor puts the card down.
                       g. Tutor goes on the next card and repeats the above procedure.

Step 4:   When tutee gives the correct response:
                       a. Tutor praises tutee.
                       b. Tutor marks the scoring sheet with a "+" next to the word.

Step 5:   At the end of the first test the tutor gives all the flash cards to the tutee to play "Game #1." The tutor asks the tutee to hand them back one at a time while identifying each word. The tutor praises each correct answer, but makes no notations on the scoring sheet.

Step 6:   The tutor gives the tutee a second test using a different group of flash cards, following the earlier procedures, and records results on the scoring sheet.

Step 7:   Following the second test, the tutor and tutee play Game #2. This is done by having the tutor lay all the cards out on the table face up so that the tutee can see them all at once. The tutor then either names a word, or gives the definition for a word. The tutee is asked to choose the correct flash card. The tutor praises the tutee's correct answers and corrects the incorrect choices. No notations are made on the scoring sheet.

Step 8:	The tutor gives the tutee a third test using the earlier procedures and records the results on the scoring sheet.
Step 9:	At the end of the tutoring session, the tutor again praises the tutee on his or her progress. Everything is put back in the tutee's folder. The tutee returns to his or her seat. The tutor reports to the teacher and shows her or him the folder.
Tutor Feedback and Monitoring:	Once each week the teacher briefly discusses the sessions with the tutor and reviews the scoring sheets. Periodically the teacher observes an entire tutoring session. From his or her notes, the teacher gives the tutor additional training and advice.

RESULTS

The effectiveness of this program is determined by the number and rate of sight vocabulary words mastered by the tutee. This tutoring program had a very positive effect on both the tutor and tutee. Tutors took their job very seriously, and tutees gained in personal self-confidence and self-esteem.

Training Case Study #4—High School Cross-Age Tutoring

Setting:	Reading Comprehension Tutoring Sixty Minutes Two Sessions per Week
Rationale for Tutoring:	High school students with serious reading problems. The students were studying to pass the State's Driver's License Exam.
Pretesting:	Low score received on test covering state's driver's manual.
Choosing the Tutor:	High school students were chosen who were good readers, had outgoing personalities, and were enthusiastic after attending a general briefing session to recruit tutors.
Training Program:	Three 60-minutes sessions Trained in praising response, recording data Signed a "tutoring contract and confidentiality statement"

Seven-Step Training Model:
Step 1:
	Check you tutor packet before each session. Make sure you have:
	  a. Data sheet
	  b. Driver's manual
	  c. Pencil
	  d. Recording sheet
	  e. Supplemental materials
	  f. Tests from file cabinet

Step 2:	Sit at the assigned table in the Special Services room.
Step 3:	Record the time and the date on the data sheet and recording sheet.
Step 4:	Take out the State Driver's Manual and the tutee's folder. Instruct the student to begin reading the manual carefully. If the tutee has trouble with any of the terms, assist in the pronunciation and definition. Have the tutee repeat the term and define it. If he or she does so correctly, say "good," "right," or "yes." If the tutee responds incorrectly, repeat the term and again have him or her respond. If the tutee responds correctly, praise him or her.
Step 5:	When the tutee gets to the materials that are highlighted or underlined, have him or her read the passages, then review the reading with the student, giving examples and explanations. Check to see if he or she understands this material is progressive. It is essential that the student fully comprehend each section in the manual.
Step 6:	Using the Tutor Log, record the date, percentage of questions answered correctly, any comments you may have, and the point in the manual where you left off (see Figure 4.10).
Step 7:	Make sure everything is placed back where it belongs so that you may find it easily for the next session.
Tutoring Session Procedures:	The State Driver's Manual is used as the basic instructional material. The tutoring objective is for the student to improve his or her reading comprehension skills so as to obtain a State Driver's Learning Permit. The tutoring program course objectives are broken down into six review areas to be tutored:

Review Area #1:

1. The tutee will identify the location of the state driver's license facility nearest his or her home.
2. The tutee will describe the limitations on a license.
3. The tutee will list the different types of licenses.
4. The tutee will describe how to reobtain his or her license if lost.
5. The tutee will understand the requirements of driver's education.
6. The tutee will list in writing the car's necessary equipment.
7. The tutee will list three reasons why a license may be revoked.

Review Area #2:

1. The tutee will state the rules of passing in traffic.
2. The tutee will list in writing six steps in passing a car.
3. The tutee will state how to use turn signals.
4. The tutee will state the different speed limits for specified areas.
5. The tutee will state how to use the different lights on the car.
6. The tutee will list in writing the five safety keys.

Review Area #3:

1. The tutee will list in writing four things one should do before driving away.
2. The tutee will describe how to watch the road when driving.
3. The tutee will describe how to respond to weather and the resulting road conditions in driving.
4. The tutee will describe how and when to use a turn signal.

```
                                  Tutor Log

Date:                    Section of Manual Read:

Tutee:                   Percentage of Questions Correctly Answered:

Tutor:                   Last Page Completed:

Comments: _____

_____

_____

_____

_____

_____

_____

_____
```

Figure 4.10. Tutor Log (Case Study 4)

5. The tutee will describe the use of the car mirrors.
6. The tutee will list in writing five things one must do to make a left turn.
7. The tutee will explain the "right of way."
8. The tutee will list in writing four turns that are not legal.
9. The tutee will describe where and how one parks a car.
10. The tutee will list in writing sixteen places where one cannot park a car.

Review Area #4:
1. The tutee will list the meanings of the different shapes and colors of road signs.
2. The tutee will describe when the driver is to stop and for whom.
3. The tutee will list some precautions to follow when driving on the interstate.
4. The tutee will describe how to use the ramps on the interstate.
5. The tutee will list in writing ten tips for safe driving on the interstate.

Review Area #5:
1. The tutee will list in writing six things that alcohol can do to one's driving skills.
2. The tutee will describe "the implied consent laws."
3. The tutee will list seven things that could get a driver into an accident.
4. The tutee will describe the procedure for a driver who has been in an accident.
5. The tutee will describe the process of registration.
6. The tutee will list in writing two things to do when selling a car.
7. The tutee will explain the meaning of different license plates.

Review Area #6:
1. The tutee will list the times for car inspection.
2. The tutee will describe how to maintain the brakes
3. The tutee will describe how to maintain the tires.
4. The tutee will list in writing three safety hints.
5. The tutee will list in writing five symbol signs.
6. The tutee will describe in writing three ways of getting information.
7. The tutee will list in writing six good driving habits that should help in getting better mileage.
8. The tutee will list in writing six ways to take care of a car.

RESULTS

This cross-age tutoring program proved very successful. A large majority of tutees were able to pass their driver's license test. Reading comprehension also increased. Tutees were highly motivated to learn something that had great practical value in an adolescent's life—driving a car. Many good peer relationships also developed between students who participated in the program.

Training Case Study #5—Junior High Classroom

Setting: Spelling Skills Tutoring
                      Sixty-Minute Sessions
                      Two Sessions per week
                      One Marking Period

Rationale for Tutoring: Junior high students who were having difficulty passing a basic spelling competencies test.

Pretesting: Spelling Basic Competency Test to determine approximate grade-level score.

Choosing the Tutor: Students with higher spelling scores.
Students who show appropriate classroom learning behaviors.

Training Program: Teacher role-played both the role of the tutor and tutee for three tutoring exercises during which the tutees would practice their spelling:
1. Single word
2. Word dictated in a sentence
3. Word in a sentence created by the tutee

Tutors and tutees then held a practice session. Teachers gave feedback through their observations.

Tutors could not begin formal tutoring sessions until they had mastered all the tutoring procedures.

Tutoring Session
Materials: Basic Competency Spelling List for pretesting (see Figure 4.11).

Tutoring Session
Procedures: Students working in partnerships exchange spelling books and take turns being "teacher" and student. The student who tutors first uses the following procedure with his or her tutee.

Keeping the record on the Spelling List Sheet, the students practice spelling words on their individual lists in three different ways:
1. The single word dictated and spelled in isolation
2. The word dictated by the tutor in a sentence; the tutee writes the sentence
3. Word given orally by the tutor and the tutee writes a sentence using the word

Dictation procedure—working with a partner.
1. Word in isolation.
   a. Tutor partner says the first word listed in his or her partner's spelling book.
   b. Tutee repeats the words and spells it aloud. If the word is spelled correctly, tutor goes on to the next step. If it is not spelled correctly, tutor gives the correct spelling, tutee repeats the word and the correct spelling.
   c. Tutee writes the word, saying each letter as he or she writes.
   d. If the tutee orally spells the word correctly and writes it correctly, the tutor enters a "+" after the word on the Spelling Data Sheet (see Figure 4.12). If the student misspells the word orally or in writing, a "0" is recorded by the tutor, and the word is studied after dictation is finished.
   e. When the tutee has three plusses in a row, the tutor draws a dark vertical line after it on the Spelling List and proceeds to sentence dictation at the next session.
2. Word in dictated sentence.
   a. Tutor dictates a sentence using the word. As many as three words from the list may be used. Remember these are only words that the tutee has mastered in isolation.
   b. Tutee repeats the sentence. If he or she does not repeat it exactly, the tutor says the sentence until the tutee can.
   c. The tutee writes the sentence. If it is helpful to do so, the tutee says each word as he or she writes it.
   d. When all the words for the day have been dictated and written in sentences, the tutor checks spelling accuracy. If the word is spelled correctly, the tutor

Words Most Frequently Misspelled in the Seventh and Eighth Grades

1. absence
2. acquaint
3. across
4. all right
5. already
6. always
7. ambition
8. among
9. answer
10. article
11. author

12. beautiful
13. because
14. before
15. begin
16. beginning
17. believe
18. benefit
19. bicycle
20. boundary
21. business
22. buy

23. captain
24. character
25. chose
26. climb
27. college
28. coming
29. cousin

30. decide
31. decided
32. decision
33. definite
34. democracy
35. democrat
36. democratic
37. describe
38. description
39. determine

40. different
41. disappear
42. disappoint
43. doctor
44. does
45. doesn't
46. dropped
47. dropping

48. every
49. exception
50. excitement
51. exciting
52. experience

53. families
54. family
55. favorite
56. February
57. fierce
58. finally
59. first
60. four
61. friend

62. getting
63. government
64. governor
65. grammar
66. guard

67. hobby
68. horse
69. hospital
70. humor

71. immediately
72. Indian
73. interesting
74. its
75. it's
76. library

77. literature
78. lose

79. meant
80. minute
81. mischievous
82. mystery

83. necessary
84. nineteen
85. ninety
86. ninth

87. occur
88. occurred
89. occurrence
90. occasionally
91. our

92. physical
93. piece
94. presents

95. quiet

96. really
97. receive
98. recommend
99. remember

100. safe
101. Saturday
102. scene
103. secretary
104. sentence
105. separate
106. separately
107. similar
108. since
109. sincere
110. sincerely
111. soldier

112. speech
113. stopped
114. stories
115. story
116. studied
117. studying
118. suggest
119. suppose
120. surprise
121. swimming

122. their
123. there
124. they're
125. thought
126. threw
127. through
128. to
129. together
130. too
131. tried
132. truly
133. two

134. until
135. unusual
136. usually

137. watch
138. weather
139. went
140. were
141. where
142. whether
143. which
144. write
145. writer
146. writing
147. written
148. wrote

149. your
150. you're

Figure 4.11. Basic Competency Spelling List

Spelling Report Sheet			

Tutee: _____

Tutor: _____

Session 1 Word List	Word in Isolation	Sentence Dictated	Word in Sentence
absence	0 + + +		
ambition	+ + +		
boundary	0 + + +		
character	+ + +		
decision	+ + +		
democracy	0 + 0 +		
exception	+ + +		
government	0 + + +		
grammar	0 0 +		
hospital	0 + + +		

Session 2 Word List	Word in Isolation	Sentence Dictated	Word in Sentence
absence		+ + +	+ + +
ambition		+ + +	0 + + +
boundary		+ + +	+ + +
character		0 + + +	+ + +
decision		+ + +	+ + +
democracy	+ + +	+ + +	0 + + +
exception		0 + + +	+ + +
government	+ + +	0 + +	
grammar	0 + + +	0 +	
hospital		0 + + +	0 +

Figure 4.12. Spelling Data Sheet

puts a plus on the chart; if misspelled, a zero. When there are three plusses in a row, the tutor draws a dark vertical line and goes on to the next step.

3. Word dictated, the tutee makes up the sentence.
   a. Tutor dictates up to three words.
   b. The tutee makes up a sentence and writes the complete sentence.
   c. When the tutee has finished writing the sentences, the tutor checks spelling and records a plus or zero. The process continues until there are three consecutive plusses.

Student partners switch roles, and the student who was the first tutor becomes the tutee; the student who was the first tutee becomes the tutor. Student partners repeat the procedure described earlier.

Monitoring: Teachers circulate while tutoring sessions are in progress:
1. Spot check words marked "mastered."
2. Students are checked on the following procedures:
   a. Giving positive feedback
   b. Giving constructive feedback, spelling rules, mnemonic devices, and so on
   c. Answering questions

RESULTS

The teacher spot checked students during monitoring. Every two weeks students were tested for mastered word spelling retention. Once a month, students were retested on the Basic Competency Test. Students who passed began working on a more difficult spelling list.

ADOPTING A TRAINING MODEL

In the last two chapters we have reviewed successful peer tutoring training procedures developed by teachers and researchers. You will undoubtedly want to combine ideas and training procedures from different models as you put together your own program.

As we have seen from the case studies in this chapter, peer tutoring and cross-age tutoring can be used for almost any subject area, grade level, and age group. Key psychology of learning principles—role-playing, behavior rehearsal, discussion, practice, and the use of checklists and tip sheets—are evident in these alternative training modes. Videotaping during your training program may also be useful for some students.

The forms we have reviewed are meant to help you as a starting point. Once your own program begins, you and your students will undoubtedly develop a variety of forms that will be useful for what you want to accomplish. Let your students become creative. With computer-assisted design, many of them may show you workable and interesting ideas that you can use to reinforce their creativity and learn something new yourself.

In the next chapter, we consider how to keep your peer tutoring program on track. How do you observe? What do you look for in student behaviors? When and how often should you conduct retraining? How do you access student and program results? These and other ongoing peer tutoring program issues will need your daily attention.

5

ASSESSMENT AND EVALUATION

As we have already seen, effective tutor training is a vital component for the success of any peer tutoring program. But this is just half the loaf.

The second major reason that peer tutoring programs fail is the lack of three essential activities:

1. Monitoring the tutors
2. Tutor retraining
3. The evaluation of results

During the tutoring sessions the teacher needs to observe the tutors and tutees frequently and assess the quality of the tutoring. This will guide tutor retraining and track the development of the tutor–tutee relationships for possible adjustments. The results of the peer tutoring program require careful evaluation to guide your future program planning.

MONITORING THE TUTORS

Four techniques for monitoring tutors can be employed.

1. Review the Tutor Diary (see Figure 3.2) that the tutors complete for each session. Check to see that it is consistent with what you are observing. Are each tutor's comments accurate? Is there a logical progression of learning activities from one class to another?
2. Provide a Tutor Guide (see Figure 5.1) that the tutors will use as job aid during each tutoring session. Let the tutors know that you will be observing these behaviors and evaluating them on accomplishing each tutoring task (see Figure 5.2).
3. Also monitor other specific essential tutoring skills that had been introduced during the tutor-training program. This will also include a rating of each tutor's personal attitude to the tutee and his or her dependability in carrying out the role of a tutor (see Figure 5.3).
4. An older student tutor may also provide valuable observations on how well the tutee is responding to their tutoring efforts (see Figure 5.4). By completing this report, the tutor can sum up how their work has progressed and ask the teacher how to overcome roadblocks that were not covered in the initial tutor-training program.

The tutor's personal evaluation can serve as a good counterbalance to your own more limited observations by revealing those tutoring areas that need additional training or by giving a red warning flag that the tutor–tutee are mismatched.

Monitoring the tutors will be effective if it is consistent and fairly administered. By using these four different monitoring techniques, the teacher will be able to arrive at a fairly balanced overview of each tutor's strengths and weaknesses.

Most student tutors take their role very seriously and want to do better. They are very sensitive to any favoritism that a teacher might show an individual student. A simple multitrack monitoring program will help you better avoid this personal pitfall and precisely target retraining areas for each tutor.

TUTOR RETRAINING

Peer tutoring programs have a greater chance of succeeding if:

1. The teacher observes the tutors as often as possible.
2. These observations help target ongoing retraining as needed.
3. The teacher maintains high motivational levels for both tutors and tutees.

Everyone likes success. Your students need constant praise and encouragement if they are to persevere and improve as tutors.

Tutoring retraining sessions should be done after the first two weeks of tutoring. This will give you enough time for ample observation and provide the students some hands-on tutoring experiences without engraining any initial bad tutoring habits.

The retraining sessions should be held as soon as possible after the daily tutoring sessions to help improve student recall and motivation. The tutors should share their experiences and pool ideas to learn from one another rather than just from you. These peer-feedback sessions are an essential part of the ongoing peer tutor training function.

The retraining class may also include the opportunity for tutors to give a short personal review of their tutoring sessions. During the following general class discussion, the teacher also has the opportunity to make suggestions based on observations made during the tutoring session. For older students a videotape of these discussions or a role-play exercise can be an added training tool for future use.

Peer tutoring can become very stressful for the tutor and tutee. Individual private coaching between the tutor and the teacher may be necessary to supplement the group training experience. However, first give the tutor's peer group the opportunity to offer their own practical suggestions for each other.

During these retraining sessions, most peer tutors will begin to learn from the teacher's observation skills and adopt them as their own. Avoid giving value judgments of "right" and "wrong" tutoring methods. Instead, discuss the cause/effect events in a typical class: What happened, and then what was the effect on the tutee's learning? This will help the tutor become more objective, better evaluate his or her own tutoring style, and try something new if it is needed to improve the tutee's learning.

As students age, they often are able to develop more personal insights into their own behavior as tutors. But students in all age groups need to be given the time and opportunity to gradually develop these critical-thinking skills. Retraining classes are one of the best arenas for facilitating the development of metacognitive skills.

EVALUATION OF RESULTS

Every peer tutoring program needs a measurement system to evaluate how well the tutees (and in most cases, the tutors) are learning. Evaluation needs to be an ongoing part of the program to assess both day-to-day student

Tutor Job Aid

Check off completion of the following tasks:

	Dates				
1. Obtain materials for class.					
2. Prepare the tutoring area.					
3. Help tutee feel comfortable					
4. Explain class objectives to the tutee.					
5. Use direction sheet to follow procedures for class.					
6. Give the tutee clear directions on how to respond to problems or questions.					
7. Praise the tutee for correct answers.					
8. If the tutee is struggling or gives a wrong answer: A. Give the correct answer & how you got it. B. Have the tutee repeat the answer.					
9. Keep accurate records of the class.					
10. End the class with positive feedback.					
11. Store the materials properly.					

Figure 5.1. Tutor Guide

Tutor Observation Checklist

Tutor: _____

Tutee: _____

Observer: _____

Tutor:
Score: "+" or "0"   *Dates Observed:*

1. Assembles material												
2. Arranges work space												
3. Explains current lesson to partner												
4. Praises correct responses												
5. Shows enthusiasm												
6. Prompts incorrect responses												
7. Uses positive manner												
8. Refers to direction sheets if needed												
9. Speaks in quiet voice												
10. Uses procedures without assistance												
11. Keeps records without assistance												
12. Replaces material at the end of session												

+ = appropriate behavior
0 = inappropriate behavior

Figure 5.2.   Tutor Observation Checklist

Tutor Skills Checklist

Tutor: _____

Observer: _____   Date: _____

	Skills Observed
	Low High
	1 2 3 4 5

A. Essential Tutoring Skills—Did the Tutor:
   1. Open the session with enthusiasm?   _____
   2. Maintain positive rapport, get and maintain tutee's attention?   _____
   3. Give clear instructions, letting tutee know precisely how she or he is to respond?   _____
   4. Give a straightforward presentation of the new information using specific examples to illustrate   _____
       a point? Speak the language correctly and appropriately?
   5. Use praise appropriately?   _____
   6. Correct the tutee by:
   • Explaining the correct answer and giving sufficient examples?   _____
   • Saying the answer with the tutee until he or she has mastered the concept?   _____
   • Requiring the tutee to say the answer alone?   _____
   • Practicing skill?   _____
   7. Avoid punishing?   _____
   8. Use appropriate cues/prompts?   _____
   9. Stay on task and pace the lesson at a reasonable pace?   _____
 10. Provide for sufficient repetition?   _____
 11. Use specific criteria to judge when an objective has been mastered?   _____
 12. Use a consistent system for reinforcement   _____

B. Dependability—Was the tutor:
   1. In attendance regularly?   _____
   2. On time?   _____
   3. Prepared with necessary student/teacher materials?   _____

C. Attitude—Was the tutor:
   1. Positive?   _____
   2. Persistent?   _____
   3. Friendly?   _____
   4. Supportive?   _____

Figure 5.3.   Sample Tutor Skills Checklist

```
                        Tutor's Summary of Tutee Response

Tutor: _____    Date: _____

Tutee: _____

Please give your viewpoints on the following points:

1. The quality of your relationship to the tutee:


2. The tutee's level of motivation:


3. The most successful use of tutoring materials:


4. The tutee's attention span:


5. General observations:


6. Questions to be resolved:
```

Figure 5.4. Sample Tutor Summary Report Form

progress and long-term achievement at the end of a semester or grading period. There are many options. Let's explore a few.

Day-to-Day Measurement

Measurable tutoring objectives established at the beginning of the tutoring program and tutor recordkeeping of the relevant data are vital for day-to-day measurement of tutoring results. Such data will allow the teacher to make accurate decisions on modifying both the tutoring and his or her own teaching content on a regular basis. (Please review some of the tutor/teacher recordkeeping forms we have already presented in the previous chapters.)

The teacher must decide:

1. What kinds of data will be kept by the tutor
2. How to evaluate whether the tutoring objectives are being met
3. What factors will trigger changes in the tutoring program

Criterion-Based Tests

An effective evaluation tool can be a test that shows student achievement in terms of their performance on a particular task measured by a standard set for that task. An example of a criterion standard is that, after a tutoring session, the student will be able to identify 90 percent of U.S. state capitals on a map. Many school districts use such criterion-referenced tests to guide day-to-day instruction toward meeting specific state-mandated learning standards. Peer tutoring can help reinforce the teaching of this information by using criterion-referenced tests and quizzes that measure the ongoing progress of the tutees.

Pre-/Postnormed Tests

School districts may wish to use normed tests at the beginning and end of each school year to help them determine annual yearly student progress. A "control group" could be established of students who did not participate in any peer tutoring activities. They could then be compared to those students at the same grade placement, aptitude, and age who were enrolled in the peer tutoring program. Other intervening variables may need to be accounted for before an accurate comparison may be made between the tutored and nontutored students. The results from this normed test data can help determine the effectiveness of the peer-tutoring program.

Evaluation Questionnaires

Test scores have serious limitations if used solely to evaluate effective learning or effective tutoring. Many students are at least partially test-phobic and, though competent learners, have emotional blocks that compromise accurate test measurement.

A primary task of evaluation is to better guide instruction in order to find out what a student knows, define strengths and weaknesses, and plan how to better individualize future learning.

The most valuable component of evaluation for a peer tutoring program can often come from the students themselves. Their feedback can come in many forms. Table 5.1, "Outline of a Plan for the Evaluation of a Peer Tutoring Program," presents a variety of methods and procedures for gathering data from students, teachers, and parents.

In addition to the data from the tutors' reports, evaluation questionnaires can provide valuable short-term and long-term information on the effectiveness of a peer-tutoring program. Both parent (see Figures 5.5a and 5.5b) and teacher (see Figures 5.6a and 5.6b) questionnaires will provide a far broader perspective on the overall short-term/long-term effects of the tutoring of an individual student. Short-term evaluations can be done one month after the conclusion of the student's peer tutoring. Long-term evaluations can be made twelve months later. For long-term evaluations, the student's current and previous teachers will be needed to complete the questionnaire.

The evaluation will give teachers an opportunity to think clearly about the short-term and long-term consequences of peer tutoring for a specific student in the classroom. If a cross-age program, the teachers of the tutee should complete the questionnaire. All of the completed questionnaires will provide invaluable qualitative data on student achievement and also provide ideas for planning as the peer-tutoring program evolves.

Portfolio Assessment

Other qualitative changes in learning can be demonstrated effectively using portfolio assessment techniques. This form of evaluation is a way of bringing together systematically gathered information and then using it to guide future instruction.

For portfolio assessment both the peer tutor and teacher take frequent samplings of the tutee's work. Observations can become a daily corrective function built into every phase of the peer tutoring program. Immediate remediation becomes the goal, rather than a reward or punishment system. Children are evaluated in terms of reaching specific learning objectives, rather than compared against each other, a class, or a hypothetical test norm.

Portfolio assessment is an organized, systematic, and gradual gathering of relevant information on the tutee's daily learning progress. If a portfolio is properly maintained by the tutor and teacher, it can be very valuable in assessing the student's development as a learner and make necessary academic programming decisions more reliable and easier to carry out.

The combined tutor, teacher, and tutee reporting forms function as a written record that filters useful and contradictory information as part of the overall evaluation process. The student's portfolio acts as both a record of results and an important quality-control management tool for the teacher.

Table 5.1. Outline of a Plan for the Evaluation of a Peer Tutoring Program

Program Evaluation Analysis Questions	Methods for Data Collection	Procedures for Data and Reporting
1. Who has participated in the tutoring program (tutors; tutees?)	Collection of demographic information and needs assessment data Preprogram data collection	Comparison of participants to expected needs and eligibility criteria
2.. How were training and supervision of tutors implemented?	Training and supervisory logs Data collection during the program	Qualitative analysis Comparison to program design expectations
3. In what manner was the tutoring program implemented?	Interviews and logs Data collection during the program	Qualitative analysis Comparison to program design expectations
4. What benefits accrued to tutors through their program participation?	Questionnaires Interviews Goal attainment ratings Data collection before, during, and after the program	Descriptive statistics Qualitative analysis Testing
5. What benefits accrued to tutees?	Questionnaires Interviews Goal attainment ratings Data collection before, during, and after the program	Qualitative analysis Testing
6. What have been reactions of teachers and parents to the program?	Interviews Questionnaires	Descriptive statistics

Adapted from: *Peer-Assisted Learning*, 1998.

Parent Evaluation of Tutoring Program

Student Name: _____ Date: _____

School: _____

Parent Name Completing Report: _____

1. What was the academic subject peer-tutored in your child's school?

2. At what level of subject proficiency and grade level was your child's performance *before* tutoring?

Proficiency Level (Circle one)	Grade Level (Fill in)
1. High	
2. Average	
3. Fair	
4. Poor	

3. *After the peer tutoring?*

Proficiency Level (Circle one)	Grade Level (Fill in)
1. High	
2. Average	
3. Fair	
4. Poor	

4. To what extent did the peer tutoring improve the student's study skills:

1	2	3	4	5
Very High	High	Moderately	Little	None

Comments:

5. To what extent did the peer tutoring improve the student's personal motivation toward academic achievement?

1	2	3	4	5
Very High	High	Moderately	Little	None

Comments:

(continued)

Figure 5.5.a. Sample Parent Short-Term Evaluation of Tutoring Program

6. To what degree is the student's success (or lack of success) in school due to the peer tutoring?

1	2	3	4	5
Very High	High	Moderately	Little	None

Comments:

7. In the future would you consider enrolling your child in a peer tutoring program?

Yes   No
Why?   Why?

8. What features of the peer tutoring program did you like most/least?

Most   Least

9. Based on your child's experience (and personal comments), what is your opinion of the educational value of our peer tutoring program?

1	2	3	4	5
Excellent	Very Good	Good	Fair	Poor

Comments:

10. What further suggestions can your offer us to improve a student's peer tutoring experience?

Figure 5.5.a.   Sample Parent Short-Term Evaluation of Tutoring Program (*continued*)

Parent Evaluation of Tutoring Program

Student Name: Date:

School:

Parent Name Completing Report:

1. What was the academic subject peer-tutored in your child's school?

2. At what level of subject proficiency and grade level was your child's performance *before* tutoring?

Proficiency Level (Circle one)	Grade Level (Fill in)
1. High	
2. Average	
3. Fair	
4. Poor	

3. One year later *After* the peer tutoring?

Proficiency Level (Circle one)	Grade Level (Fill in)
1. High	
2. Average	
3. Fair	
4. Poor	

4. One year after the peer tutoring experience, to what degree has the student's study:

I	2	3	4	5
Very High	High	Moderately	Little	None

Comments:

5. One year after the peer tutoring experience, to what degree has the student's personal motivation toward academic achievement?

I	2	3	4	5
Very High	High	Moderately	Little	None

Comments:

(continued)

Figure 5.5.b.   Sample Parent Long-Term Evaluation of Tutoring Program

6. One year after the peer tutoring experience, to what degree do you credit this program for the student's success (or lack of success) in school?

I	2	3	4	5
Very High	High	Moderately	Little	None

Comments:

7. In the future would you consider enrolling the student in another peer-tutoring program?

Yes   No
Why?   Why?

8. What features of the peer-tutoring program did you like most/least?

Most   Least

9. Based on your child's experience (and personal comments), what is your opinion of the educational value of our peer tutoring program?

I	2	3	4	5
Excellent	Very Good	Good	Fair	Poor

Comments:

10. What further suggestions can your offer us to improve a student's peer tutoring experience?

Figure 5.5.b.   Sample Parent Long-Term Evaluation of Tutoring Program (*continued*)

Teacher Evaluation of Tutoring Program

Student Name: Date:

School:

Teacher:

1. What was the academic subject(s) peer tutored for this student?

2. At what level of subject proficiency and grade-level attainment was the student's performance *before* tutoring?

Proficiency Level (Circle one)   *Grade Level (Fill in)*

1. High

2. Average

3. Fair

4. Poor

3. *After* the peer tutoring?

Proficiency Level (Circle one)   *Grade Level (Fill in)*

1. High

2. Average

3. Fair

4. Poor

4. To what extent did the peer tutoring improve the student's daily academic classroom performance?

1	2	3	4	5
Very High	High	Moderately	Little	None

Comments:

5. To what extent did the peer tutoring improve the student's personal motivation toward academic achievement?

1	2	3	4	5
Very High	High	Moderately	Little	None

Comments:

(continued)

Figure 5.6.a.   Sample Teacher Short-Term Evaluation of Tutoring Program

6. To what degree did the student's overall achievement improve due to the peer tutoring?

1	2	3	4	5
Very High	High	Moderately	Little	None

Comments:

7. In the future would this student benefit from additional peer tutoring? (Circle one)

Yes   No
Why?   Why?

8. What features of the peer tutoring program were most beneficial or least beneficial for this student?

Most   Least

9. Based on this student's peer tutoring enrollment, what was the overall effect of peer tutoring on increasing academic achievement?

1	2	3	4	5
Excellent	Very Good	Good	Fair	Poor

Comments:

10. Further comments and suggestions:

Figure 5.6.a. Sample Teacher Short-Term Evaluation of Tutoring Program (*continued*)

Teacher Evaluation of Prior Year Tutoring Program

Student Name: Date:

School:

Teacher (Previous School Year):

Teacher (Current School Year):

1. What was the academic subject(s) peer tutored for this student?

2. Last year, what was the level of subject proficiency and grade-level attainment of the student *before* the peer tutoring?

Proficiency Level (Circle one)	Grade Level (Fill in)
1. High	
2. Average	
3. Fair	
4. Poor	

3. For this school year?

Proficiency Level (Circle one)	Grade Level (Fill in)
1. High	
2. Average	
3. Fair	
4. Poor	

4. For the current school year, to what extent has the peer tutoring improved the student's daily academic classroom performance?

1	2	3	4	5
Very High	High	Moderately	Little	None

Comments:

5. For the current school year, to what extent has the peer tutoring improved the student's personal motivation toward academic achievement?

1	2	3	4	5
Very High	High	Moderately	Little	None

Comments:

(continued)

Figure 5.6.b.   **Sample Teacher Long-Term Evaluation of a Tutoring Program**

6. One year after the peer tutoring experience, to what degree has the student's overall achievement improved?

1	2	3	4	5
Very High	High	Moderately	Little	None

Comments:

7. For the current school year, is this student enrolled in a peer tutoring program? (Circle one)

Yes   No
Why?   Why?

8. What features of last year's peer tutoring program were most beneficial or least beneficial for this student?

Most   Least

9. For the current school year, what has been the overall effect of peer tutoring on increasing this student's academic achievement?

1	2	3	4	5
Excellent	Very Good	Good	Fair	Poor

Comments:

10. Further comments and suggestions:

Figure 5.6.b. Sample Teacher Long-Term Evaluation of a Tutoring Program (*continued*)

Student portfolios also help provide tutees with physical evidence of what they have learned and support their experience of positive accomplishment. Research shows that these portfolios can often become a mechanism for helping students to become truly independent classroom learners. They also aid teachers in better facilitating individualized student learning.

EVALUATION—THE BOTTOM LINE

Optimal evaluations of peer tutoring program results will track four levels of student learning:

1. New skills learning
2. Student mastery over information
3. Acquisition of higher level thinking skills (metacognition)
4. Formation of independent learning (i.e., planning how to learn)

As our review of learning assessment and program evaluation has shown, it appears that there are multiple pathways for gathering such information. The teacher needs both quantitative and qualitative data to measure student/program results. This information will help the teacher to make future tutoring instruction improvements, as well as strengthen long-term support for peer tutoring among fellow teachers, the school administration, and the students' parents.

In the next chapter, we present a case-study overview of results from a wide diversity of peer/cross-age tutoring programs.

SUCCESS STORIES:
"THE IQ IS OFTEN LESS IMPORTANT
IN ANY PERSON'S EDUCATION
THAN THE 'I WILL!'"

OVERCOMING OBJECTIONS

Despite the general belief by most classroom teachers that one-to-one instruction is the best of all possible teaching methods, peer tutoring has usually been ignored because of several general assumptions:

1. Student tutors cannot be trained in an effective programmed tutoring format that will profitably supplement the classroom teacher's instruction.
2. Peer tutoring is too expensive!
3. Peer tutoring takes too much teacher time to implement.
4. Little research has been published supporting the effectiveness of peer tutoring.

As we have already seen, student tutors can be properly trained to become effective peer tutors. In the past twenty-five years, many different training models have been researched and proven effective for student peer or cross-age tutors. From the training information we have reviewed, most teachers can easily design and implement a tutoring program for their own classroom or a collaborative cross-age tutoring program with another teacher.

The cost of using nonpaid student tutors is very low. Moreover, research has shown that when such tutoring is provided, it can be several times as cost-effective as conventional teaching alone. However, the cost-effectiveness of peer tutoring depends heavily on the effectiveness of the program's management system (planning, training, monitoring, evaluation).

If teachers learn to use proven peer tutoring management best practices, the investment of their professional time will be kept to a minimum. One of the chief goals of this resource guide is to help you adapt this information for local classroom use and avoid the costly time investment of reinventing the wheel.

Since the 1960s, comprehensive research has been published on the practical use of peer or cross-age tutoring. Peer tutoring can have extremely positive results on student learning and significantly raise the reading comprehension scores of tutees. Let us now explore the final dimension of successfully implementing your own peer tutoring program through an overview of published research results.

WHY TUTORING SUCCEEDS

Research shows that the current interest in peer/cross-tutoring focuses on two main issues:

1. The success of peer tutoring as a supplemental classroom learning strategy
2. The use of peer tutoring to help teachers better understand what students know and how they come to understand it

Cognitive and metacognitive processing is at the heart of peer tutoring. Tutors are required to explain the knowledge they have acquired. Thus, peer tutoring gives teachers realistic glimpses into how their students think, otherwise remains largely hidden.

Stanford University researchers (1984) Levin, Glass, and Meister used standardized tests in reading and math to rank performance improvement of four learning strategy alternatives: computer-based instruction (CBI), reduced class size, cross-age tutoring, and increased teacher instructional time. The results ranked cross-age tutoring as most effective over all the other options. In addition, they found that cross-age tutoring was nearly four times more cost-effective than reducing class size or increasing instructional time.

Charles Jones (1981) conducted an eight-year study of sixth- and seventh-grade Michigan tutors and tutees in a remedial reading comprehension program. The tutoring followed a highly structured cross-age tutoring program. Both tutors and tutees made significant reading gains over and above normal classroom instruction. Tutees' mean gains were statistically significant over the five-year period.

However, in research conducted by Mary Rogers (1969), a tutorial reading program pairing sixth-grade underachievers and third-grade remedial readers failed to yield positive achievement gains. The third-graders made gains in reading scores that were significant. However, the sixth-graders tested just as well as the control group that did not act as tutors. This was the result of two significant program weaknesses.

1. The short length of the tutoring training program
2. The curriculum used for tutoring was unstructured and not prepared on a programmable basis

These factors led to poor reading results for the tutors. Douglas Robertson (1971) later reinforced these conclusions when he replicated the results in a similar study of a fifth-grade peer tutoring program. If tutors are not given extensive training both before and during the tutoring program, there is a significant risk that either the tutors or the tutees or both will not make significant gains in reading achievement.

Underachieving African American male tutors and tutees in a study by Eileen Liette (1971) showed significant gains in reading achievement. This peer tutoring program for all subjects was highly structured. Personal motivation and learner self-confidence improved. These motivational changes occurred prior to personal growth in reading achievement.

Mary Hallick's (1974) study of a second- and seventh-grade cross-age tutoring program in reading failed to produce gains in reading achievement, though she found some improvement in student self-confidence. Program failings included:

1. No initial diagnostic testing
2. Tutoring sessions were far too short
3. Initial tutor training was insufficient and had no subsequent retraining cycle

Carole Bernstein's (1979) similar findings affirms that the techniques and materials used to train tutors must be skill specific, feature tutor behavior programming, and offer a retraining feature.

Indeed, if training, curriculum programming, and tutor materials are carefully planned and implemented, Velma Moore's (1978) research confirms that peer tutoring can effectively improve reading achievement and learner self-image. Her study in Texas accounted for these tutoring program variables using 188 sixth-, fifth-, and second-grade cross-age tutors. It showed significant statistical gains in posttest reading comprehension and vocabulary.

Judy Rogers (1969) studied such a highly structured cross-age reading program that featured sixth-grade students tutoring first-graders in phonics. The students scored reading gains. She also found that if upper-grade elementary students are properly trained, they could be cost-effective in tutoring primary-grade children in reading. Many other cross-age tutoring studies also agree that it is one of the most feasible approaches for providing effective individualized instruction to primary grade children.

From a different vantage point, Rosemary Hoing (1980) conducted a research study on cross-age tutoring in reading by fourth-graders for first-graders. She measured the reading improvement of the tutors rather than the tutees. She also found that a highly organized and administered tutoring program produced significant reading achievement gains by the fourth-grade tutors. The tutor's self-concept was also improved significantly.

Other factors that Rogers found influenced successful outcomes of student tutorial reading programs included frequent school–home communication on the positive nature of the tutoring session. This established a positive supporting attitude from the student's parents. The perception of academic improvement by parents was, in the long run, as important as the reading improvement itself.

According to Rogers, school scheduling policies also need reappraisal to facilitate the bringing together of students of different ages and grade levels. In traditional schools, certain subjects are taught at the same time, regardless of grade level. This allows the students to move from one grade to another without disruption. In ungraded or nontraditional schools, a learning resource center or procedure was established to allow older students to be available to work with younger students.

Research by Linda Ronshi (1974) showed the effectiveness of using learning-disabled peer and cross-age student tutoring in reading. She discovered that if properly trained and given a structured reading program, these tutors also profited from the tutoring experience. Cross-age tutoring reduced these students' cultural, generation gap, and authority barriers to personal communications. It enhanced their ego development and self-esteem. Student tutors saw a new use for learning subject matter that also helped their own assimilation of new information and aroused personal interest in a subject area. The cross-age tutors' tutoring experience allowed them to practice adult teacher roles and visualize the possibilities of their own place in society as an adult. For many cross-age tutors, their learning behavior improved simply because, for the first time their lives, they were placed in a position of trust and responsibility. Once this process began, a self-perpetuating cycle kicked in. The students felt good about themselves. This lowered the personal risk of failure in learning something new.

THE MAGICAL WORDS: PEER TUTORING

Other at-risk student populations also seem to respond positively to tutoring. One such example is Jean Bond's (1982) study of using persistent high school truants to tutor elementary school children, ages five to eight, who had been identified as "slow learners" by their teacher. In this cross-age tutoring program, adolescents who showed little or no interest in learning, did not value education, and had very low achievement levels were chosen as tutors.

These tutors attended an alternative education program for persistent truants operated by the Coventry City Council in the United Kingdom. This program was staffed by instructors from the University of Warwick. Each tutor attended eight, 2.5-hour training sessions. The Truancy Centre program offered the cross-age tutoring for one and a half days per week for two school terms. Each tutor was responsible for instructing two of the younger students.

For this mix of these problematic students, peer tutoring seemed to work like magic as these tutees were virtually transformed before the teachers' eyes. However, this Warwick program is not a unique formula. Other peer/cross-age tutoring efforts have shown similar evidence in changing at-risk adolescents' attitudes toward learning. In this study, Bond noted improvement in:

- Basic skills in reading and writing
- The students' understanding of subject areas
- The students' self-image
- The students' attitude toward school, learning, and teachers
- The students' understanding of child-rearing practices

The research evidence showed that almost all of the truant adolescents in the cross-age tutoring program were markedly transformed into reliable, conscientious, caring individuals who became concerned about the educational progress of their tutees. They even began to sympathize, to some degree, with their own teachers and began to develop some personal insight into their own educational programs. Evidence from this and other at-risk cross-age tutoring programs indicate that everyone wins. Tutors and tutees benefit as well as the teachers of the tutors.

TUTORING AS THERAPY

Douglas G. Ellson has been one of America's leading researchers on the strategies and benefits of peer/cross-age tutoring. A summary research study conducted by Ellson and colleagues (1965) explored the results of ten programs that had tutored over 400 children. These included mentally challenged students, slow learners, and pupils in kindergarten and first grade.

Ellson and colleagues' report showed that peer tutoring combined with classroom instruction was more effective than classroom instruction alone. Peer tutoring had a "therapeutic" effect by helping students recall earlier classroom teaching. It also provided children time to demonstrate learning behaviors and abilities modeled on their tutor or teacher. In some cases, these authors also found that these favorable effects extended to attitudes and behavior outside of school.

Though Ellson and colleagues found large differences between the different groups of children, these differences were more pronounced at the beginning of the peer tutoring program. After an initial period in which individual differences were prominent, most students (except the mentally challenged pupils) came to learn at about the same rate as the faster learners. Ellson and colleagues further believe that peer tutoring programs can be programmed to account for individual learning needs. They, for example, can help overcome the failure of learning to read that some students experience through group teaching in the classroom.

RESCUED FOR THE FUTURE

Another cross-age tutoring program was studied by Cloward (1967) in which tenth- and eleventh-grade students from an economically distressed urban neighborhood tutored low-achieving fourth- and fifth-grade pupils reading below grade level. The tutors were paid for their training and tutoring services. The two-hour tutoring sessions were held three days per week. Each student was assigned a specific tutor. Tutoring took place in local school classrooms. The tutor escorted the pupil home at the end of each session.

Two-hundred-forty tutors participated in this program. Most of the tutors were females reading at the tenth-grade level, though 22 percent read below the eighth-grade level. All the tutors received four afternoons of training a week for a two-week period.

This tutoring program showed that if emphasis is placed on individual attention and basic skills training, academically problematic students can make substantial progress in reading. However, this improvement for the tutee may not become evident during the period of tutoring, but only later as the student progresses through school.

The greatest impact of this cross-age program was on the tutors themselves. Becoming tutors improved their personal self-concept as learners. This helped students overcome the alienation from school that arose from prior failure and humiliation in the classroom. With proper supervision and training, potential high school dropouts can improve their own academic skills and be rescued from a potentially bleak future.

A NEW "TEAM" EFFORT

American popular culture is greatly influenced by team sports. Reading researcher Connie Juel (1999) discovered almost by accident how to mobilize this popular interest to increase student motivation.

A graduate student at the University of Texas at Austin was tutoring special-education children in reading at a local elementary school. She was also tutoring student athletes at the university. One day she brought one of these college athletes to a tutoring session. "A magical thing happened. The special education student tried harder than ever, and Calvin (the athlete) began working with him."

Because of his power as a role model, this student made strides with Calvin that even a talented tutor had been unable to produce. Calvin also enjoyed the new personal experience of making a positive difference in a child's life. He continued to volunteer at this school for over a year.

Thus a program was born in which the tutors were college athletes who had scored poorly on the Nelson-Denny reading test administered by the athletic department. Many of these students had been admitted to the university more on the basis of their athletic skills than their academic record.

In preparation for the tutoring program, the student athletes read self-selected novels and completed extensive writing assignments in personal journals. They also received tutor training in reading.

Tutor athletes then were assigned to work with one student for a forty-five-minute session twice each week. The children were in first and second grade, and in special education. Once each week, the tutors attended an evening literacy and tutor-training class in which they learned how to become better tutors for basic reading skills.

The first cross-age tutoring program enrolled twenty first-grade children, all in the lowest reading groups in their classes. By the end of the semester-long program, eighteen of the twenty students had moved to a higher reading group. Only two students were retained. All of the teachers noted that the children's confidence levels had been boosted by the tutor athletes. One first-grade teacher noted:

The kids go to tutoring and come back with their chests all puffed out. They feel so special that someone cares enough about them to come and work with them. All of their reading has improved. Their self-confidence has improved.

Another teacher wrote:

I have seen students involved in tutoring not only improve their reading skills, but gain self-confidence throughout all of their academic pursuits. Having someone besides their teacher to be interested in their progress, to listen to them read, and most of all to care about what they have to say, has made an observable difference in their academic and personal life.

Student self-confidence also spread across all subject areas. A first-grade teacher described the academic growth of one girl:

She is more outgoing than I've ever seen her. She participates in all class discussions. She used to sit there sullenly—wouldn't even participate when called on. I've never had an improvement like that before. She looks forward to his coming now and asks when he is coming. She even drew him a picture of a rainbow. Before, I could never get her to finish anything. Now I wish you could see her papers in math and social studies. I could cry I'm so happy about it. Now she asks if she can stay after school and read with me. I couldn't get her to write her name before and now she is writing cards to her mom and to James (her tutor).

The tutoring's achievement effects even spread to areas of student interest that had little to do with the classroom. A second-grade teacher commented:

The tutor took Adam to the school library and they checked out all the books on filmmaking. Adams's so excited. He's been telling me all about how movies are made. He also is writing a movie script with his tutor. He says he wants to be a film writer.

Teachers were amazed when parents who never came to school voluntarily showed up to tell them how much their children benefited from their tutors:

His mother came in at lunch to tell me that she sees a difference in him. He has learned to read much better, is more self-confident. Mom says she has to make him put his reading books away so that he will do the rest of his homework. She never saw him read before.

There were many reasons for the success of this athlete-based cross-age tutoring program. Most of the tutors had experienced academic problems in the past or present. They could easily relate to their students. One student athlete wrote, "Jonathan is having problems in school just as I did at his age."

Many of the tutors had been embarrassed as children because of their poor reading skills. Others had been told by teachers they were "stupid" or "that I wasn't smart enough to go to college." So the athletes became role models for their students, not just in reading but also in succeeding in school and life. Some even brought their tutees to the college campus to show them around.

The fact that these tutors were minority males was also extremely powerful for these children. Many were being raised in single-parent families by their mothers. Several mothers told the school's teachers about how good a role model the male tutors were for their children.

Another positive benefit of this program was that athletes who had trouble learning to read began to understand where, how, and why reading problems can occur. During the ongoing tutoring training, some college students recalled visual or auditory perceptual problems they had experienced as students. This reinforced their understanding of why it was so important to help a child overcome these same issues.

The cross-age tutoring process works because the tutors gain positive self-esteem from their role as teachers. Their own cognitive self-development is aided as they focus on the learning process of another person. They then can internalize the tutoring/learning process as it applies to them. In preparing the tutoring materials, they spend much more time on the learning task than they would just doing their own school-related assignments.

HIGH SCHOOL MATH

Anne Grossman and H. H. Lehman (1985) studied a completely different application of peer tutoring in a high school math program that included fifty sophomores in a prealgebra course. The math class used a double period with the combination of a forty-minute teaching class followed by a forty-minute peer tutoring class.

The focus of the tutoring session was on correcting errors made on a formative math test. Each tutor was paired with a tutee who had failed to answer correctly 85 percent of the test items. The tutoring activity occurred between the taking of the test and a later retest.

Almost every student had some opportunity to be a tutor, since not every student scored well on every test. The tutors developed a deeper understanding of math concepts. In general, all the students increased their sense of "math security" and a belief in their abilities to learn mathematics.

By the end of the school year, 76 percent of the students who had participated in the peer tutoring program passed the state math examination, compared with 46 percent in the entire school.

A VARIETY OF SOLUTIONS

From the research case studies cited earlier, we can see that successful peer/cross-age tutoring applications come in all shapes and sizes. Many elementary, high school, and college students improved their basic skills, achievement ability, metacognitive skills, learning behaviors, and intrinsic and extrinsic motivation regarding schooling, learning, and sometimes life itself.

A substantial amount of research stretching back forty years shows how and why typical classroom teachers have profitably used these programs. Now that we have presented all of the components of peer tutoring, there remain few reasons for you not to try it yourself!

In the last chapter, we review some strategies to obtain and retain ongoing support for a peer tutoring program. Students, parents, administrators, and teachers all need to see why they should continue their support of classroom peer tutoring or interclass/interschool cross-age tutoring programs.

7

FINDING LONG-TERM SUPPORT

People who say it cannot be done, should not interrupt people doing it.

—Chinese Proverb

Teachers across America have witnessed the extensive educational benefits for students participating in peer/cross-age tutoring programs. There seem to be few, if any, boundary lines limiting the academic areas in which students can tutor other students.

A national survey of U.S. tutoring during a typical school year conducted by this author found that peer/cross-age tutoring represents only about ten percent of all the tutoring programs provided across America. This underlines the unfortunate fact that very few teachers and schools make use of these programs. Why? Because almost everyone sees problems: matching timetables, moving pupils between classrooms, not enough time for planning and training, and the outcry of parents that student tutors are missing their own lessons working with a "tutee."

As we have seen, these objections have been repeatedly laid to rest in the persuasive research on peer/cross-age tutoring published over the past forty years. In order to obtain and retain solid support for your peer tutoring program, there are five groups you will need to influence:

1. School administrators
2. Other teachers
   • At your school
   • At other schools: elementary, secondary, college/university
3. Parents
4. Students
5. Yourself

Let's review how to motivate each of these groups.

SCHOOL ADMINISTRATORS

In this new era of educational accountability, peer/cross-age tutoring provides one answer to the question, "What proven, underutilized, cost-effective resource already exists within the educational system that can help schools help themselves?"

A Stanford University study (1984) by Levin, Glass, and Meister of peer math and reading tutoring showed that it was:

- Two times more cost-effective as computer-based instruction (CBI)
- Three times more cost-effective than lengthening the school day or reducing class size

You can help administrators review this and other research with similar results indicating that peer tutoring can be proven to be extremely cost-effective, yet yield strong achievement results when compared to other instructional alternatives.

Also, peer tutoring yields an exponential increase of school "help-giving resources" in a cost-effective way. Why? Because peer tutoring helps mobilize the "school's ethos." In other words, it promotes a cultural norm of helping, caring, and involving everyone in an educational experience. Peer tutoring is based on the concept of the school as a "learning community" and helps counter a popular culture of indifference to the needs of other people. It assists administrators and teachers in unlocking the true learning potential of every student in any school.

Another aspect of tutoring that administrators will view as a benefit is that peer/cross-age tutoring programs can be a means for diminishing teacher isolation and fostering an instructional team approach to learning. Such programs can bring teachers together for mutual support and problem solving. These programs provide a "neutral place" for teachers to expand their own pool of instructional ideas, materials, and methods. Peer tutoring programs can act as an in-school community service forum that strengthens classroom learning through the personal and social development of students.

OTHER TEACHERS

For teachers tutoring can be an important means of introducing or expanding active learning in the classroom. Peer tutoring can help teachers change the "learning culture" of a classroom and the day-to-day nature of the educational endeavor. As we have seen, it can assist students in developing their character, intellect, sense of citizenship, and the values of equality, cooperation, and caring. Students often show a greater liking for school, greater concern for others, greater enjoyment of helping others learn, and increase their own academic self-esteem.

Peer tutoring programs help teachers establish their own support groups. Teachers can meet to break down peer isolation, coach others, and develop innovative partnerships among individuals and schools. Tutoring programs also can enable teachers to exchange ideas, techniques, and success stories in an often low-risk, informal environment.

As peer tutoring programs mature, there are few limits to how they will grow and develop once teachers' imaginations take over. Many expand from basic reading, spelling, or math skill-building programs to more complex areas of learning in science, history, geography, current events, music, art, dance, computer assisted instruction, test-taking, writing, research papers, using the Internet/library for research, and many other learning activities.

PARENTS

For parents, as we have seen, it is important to stress the "double benefit" of peer tutoring. Both the tutor and tutee gain from the learning experience. Tutoring helps students cultivate better listening and communication skills. Research tells us that we learn:

- 10 percent of what we READ
- 20 percent of what we HEAR
- 30 percent of what we SEE
- 50 percent of what we both SEE and HEAR
- 70 percent of what we DISCUSS with others
- 80 percent of what we READ and EXPERIENCE personally
- 90 percent of what we TUTOR/TEACH others.

For parents, the bottom line is that as a tutor their child will gain a deeper understanding of a skill or subject by trying to explain it in a way that makes sense to a peer or a younger student. The training to become a peer tutor and the practice as a tutor teaches important higher level thinking skills. "Learning how to learn" is at the heart of peer tutoring and good schooling and is an important life skill.

STUDENTS

Most students see themselves as "nonparticipants" when it comes to the subject of learning in school. Only "nerds," "geeks," and the "totally noncool" ever get excited or enthusiastic about school, learning, books, reading, and so on. Unfortunately, more than ever, this seems deeply ingrained in today's youth culture. Many teachers have given up trying to influence or change the majority of their students' attitudes toward learning.

The key for a teacher to break through this popular culture roadblock to learning is to shift the focus of learning from the teacher back to the students, where it belongs. As we have reviewed the great diversity of peer tutoring programs, it is startling that such a wide variety of students ever got involved.

The secret to peer tutoring success is its self-actualizing power for the ordinary child or adolescent. This is part of the constructivist approach to learning. For the first time, most of these students experience being needed, valued, and respected by another person in their new role as a tutor. This helps activate the tutor's "emotional intelligence," producing a new view of self as a worthwhile human being. Many students can begin seeing themselves as givers and helpers rather than the passive "victims" in the "learning prison" of school.

There are many ways to unlock the motivational power of peer tutoring. We have outlined different tutor training programs that offer you several alternatives for use with your best, average, and most challenging students. Your use of both extrinsic rewards (public recognition, certificates, giving extra time for independent activities, etc.) and intrinsic rewards (allowing a problematic student to become a peer/cross-age tutor; giving students the ability to plan, select, and use different tutoring strategies; allowing tutors to cross-train each other; letting tutors execute independent learning projects with their tutee, etc.) will have a powerful influence over how much new learning results from the program.

YOURSELF

We have attempted to present in a useable way instructional methods for you to make practical use of peer or cross-age tutoring in your classroom. These programs are not magic bullets that will solve all your classroom instructional issues, but they can become educational methods for effectively reinforcing your daily classroom teaching.

To provide you with self-motivation for the long term, I have drawn up the following list of results that you might expect from using peer/cross-age tutoring activities in your classroom.

- Peer tutors help fashion new learning ideas from what the teacher has presented to the class that help tutees build on this new knowledge or restructure their current knowledge.

- Tutors and tutees are given frequent opportunities to engage, to varying degrees, in complex, meaningful, problem-based activities.
- Tutoring provides students with a variety of information resources and tools to make new learning personally meaningful and understandable.
- Tutors and tutees work collaboratively and engage in task-oriented conversation with one another, increasing the depth of their understanding.
- Tutors make their own thinking processes understandable to tutees and encourage others to do the same through dialogue, writing, hands-on projects, or other means.
- Tutors are ultimately encouraged to focus beyond getting the "right answer" with the tutees, and instead to explain ideas, interpret meaning, answer the "why" in explanations that seek to solve "problems."
- Tutoring encourages all students to think more deeply and develop independent ideas.
- Teachers develop a variety of learning assessment strategies through tutoring. These record how well students understand ideas, give feedback on student learning, and offer concrete examples of student thinking skills.

These opportunities for student academic growth are realistic. To develop your own program, you simply need to select from the wide variety of peer tutoring methods we have reviewed. Once you get your feet wet, you will probably want to retain this powerful instructional tool in your personal teaching tool kit—year after year.

I only have one final question to ask: Who are you? If you see yourself as a coach, a mentor, and a guide to learning—then peer tutoring is for you. You can use peer tutoring to help make students your active allies in the pursuit of knowledge. The average child in the twenty-first century will require more skills, knowledge, and understanding to have a successful life than the average child required in the twentieth century. Peer tutoring is an important curriculum tool that will help you better unlock the doors of learning to this flood of new knowledge that your students must assimilate to grow and prosper in our high-tech, global society.

BIBLIOGRAPHY

Over the past forty years an extensive body of literature has been developed on peer/cross-age tutoring. The following bibliography offers teachers just a small sampling of the books, articles, and dissertations available about tutoring. They will give you more details, ideas, and tutoring methods should you choose to invest the research time to enrich your peer tutoring program. If you have any questions as you conduct your research, you can contact the author at www.tutorquest.info. Good luck!

Abrams, L. M., Pedulla, J. J., & Madaus, G. F. (2003). Views from the classroom: Teachers' opinions of statewide testing programs. *Theory into Practice, 42*(1), 18–29.

Barksdale-Ladd, M. A., & Thomas, K. F. (2000). What's at stake in high-stakes testing: Teachers and parents speak out. *Journal of Teacher Education, 51*(5), 384–397.

Bernstein, C. E. (1979). *The effects of cross-age tutoring on elementary-level tutors and tutees.* Unpublished doctoral dissertation. Coral Gables, FL: University of Miami.

Bloom, B. S. (1984). The search for methods of group instruction as effective as one-to-one tutoring. *Educational Leadership, 41*(8), 4–16.

Bond, J. (1982). Pupil tutoring: The educational conjuring trick. *Educational Review, 34*(3), 241–252.

Cloward, R. D. (1967). Studies in tutoring. *Journal of Experimental Education, 36*(1), 14–25.

Cremin, L. A. (1964). *The transformation of the school.* New York: Vintage Books.

Ellson, D. G. (1976). Tutoring. In: *The psychology of teaching methods* (pp. 130–165). Chicago: University of Chicago Press.

Ellson, D. G., Barber, L., Engle, T. L., & Kampwert, L. (1965). Programmed tutoring: A teaching aid and a research tool. *Reading Research Quarterly, 1*(1), 77–121.

Gordon, E. E., & Gordon, E. H. (1990). *Centuries of tutoring: A history of alternative education in America and western Europe.* Lanham, MD: University Press of America.

———. (2003). *Literacy in America: Historic journey and contemporary solutions.* Westport, CT: Praeger.

———. (2002). *Tutor quest: Finding effective education for children and adults.* Bloomington, IN: Phi Delta Kappa Educational Foundation.

Grossman, A. S., & Lehman, H. H. (1985). Mastery learning and peer tutoring in a special program. *Mathematics Teacher, 78*(1), 24–27.

Harrison, G. V., & Guymon, R. E. (1980). *Structured tutoring.* Englewood Cliffs, NJ: Educational Technology Publications.

Hallick, M. P. (1974). *A study of the effects of a tutoring program on the reading achievement of seventh grade students engaged in tutoring second grade students.* Unpublished doctoral dissertation. Milwaukee: Marquette University.

Herman, J. L., & Golan, S. (1991). *Effects of standardized testing on teachers and learning: Another look* (CSE Technical Report 334). Los Angeles: University of California, National Center for Research on Evaluation, Standards, and Student Testing.

Hoing, R. J. (1980). *The effects of intergrade tutoring on fourth grade tutors in the areas of reading achievement and attitude.* Unpublished doctoral dissertation. Waco, Texas: Baylor University.

James, W. (1901). *Talks to teachers on psychology: And to students on some of life's ideals.* New York: Henry Holt.

Johnston, P. (1998). The consequences and the use of standardized tests. In: S. Murphy (Ed.), *Fragile evidence: A critique of reading assessment* (pp. 89–101). Mahwah, NJ: Lawrence Erlbaum.

Jones, C. P. Jr. (1981). *A descriptive study of cross-age peer tutoring as a strategy for reading improvement in two selected middle schools of the Highland Park Michigan system 1970 to 1978.* Unpublished doctoral dissertation. Detroit Michigan: Wayne State University.

Juel, C. (1999). Cross-age tutoring between student athletes and at-risk children. *The Reading Teacher, 45*(3), 178–186.

Levin, H. M., Glass, G. V., and Meister, G. R. (1984). *The cost–effectiveness of four educational interventions.* Stanford, CA: The University Institute for Research on Educational Finance and Governance (ERIC Document Reproduction Service No. ED 246 533).

Liette, E. E. (1971). *Tutoring: Its effects on reading achievement, standard-setting and affect-mediating self-evaluation for black male underachievers in reading.* Unpublished doctoral dissertation. Cleveland, OH: Case Western Reserve University.

McNeil, L. M. (2000). *Contradictions of school reform: Educational costs of standardized testing.* New York: Routledge.

Melaragno, R. J. (1976). The tutorial community. In: V. L. Allen (Ed.), *Children as teachers: Theory and research on tutoring* (pp. 189–197). New York: Academic Press.

Moore, V. E. T. (1978). *The effects of cross-age tutoring on elementary level tutors and tutees.* Unpublished doctoral dissertation. College Station, Texas: East Texas State University.

Pierce, M.M., Stahlbrand, K., and Armstrong, S.B (1984). *Increasing student productivity through peer tutoring programs.* Austin: Pro-Ed.

Robertson, D. J. (1971). *The effects of an intergrade tutoring experiment on tutor attitudes and reading achievement.* Unpublished doctoral dissertation. Salem: University of Oregon.

Rogers, J. (1979). *The effects of tutoring by sixth graders on the reading performance of first graders.* Unpublished doctoral dissertation. San Francisco: University of San Francisco.

Rogers, M. S. (1969). *A study of an experimental tutorial reading program in which sixth-grade underachievers tutoring third-grade children who were experiencing difficulty in reading.* Unpublished doctoral dissertation. Tuscaloosa: University of Alabama.

Ronshi, L. D. (1974). *The effects of cross-age tutors on selected personality factors of LD students.* Unpublished master's thesis. Chicago: DePaul University.

Rose, L. C. (2004). No Child Left Behind: The mathematics of guaranteed failure. *Educational Horizons, 82*(2), 121–130.

Smith, M. L. (1991). Put to the test: The effects of external testing on teachers. *Educational Researcher, 20*(5), 8–11.

Topping, K. & Ehly, S. (eds.). (1998). *Peer Assisted Learning.* Mahwah, NJ: L. Erlbaum Associates.

ABOUT THE AUTHOR

Edward E. Gordon has conducted tutoring research and practice for over thirty years. While teaching in early childhood education at DePaul University, Chicago, Dr. Gordon developed a field-based mastery-learning, diagnostic-development tutoring program used with over 10,000 children. Later while teaching in adult education/workplace literacy at Loyola University, Chicago, he expanded the tutoring model for use by 20,000 adults. In 1982, the North Central Association of Colleges and Schools (NCA) accredited this tutoring program. As a result Dr. Gordon has provided faculty in-service programs on teacher-conducted tutoring and student peer tutoring to schools across the United States.

Dr. Gordon's tutoring research for children has been published in such books as *Tutor Quest: Finding Effective Education for Children and Adults* and *Centuries of Tutoring, Literacy in America: Historic Journey and Contemporary Solutions*, and for adults in *FutureWork, Closing the Literacy Gap in American Business*, and *Skills Wars*. Gordon's work on tutoring also has been featured in the *Phi Delta Kappan, Principal Leadership, Education Update* (Association for Supervision and Curriculum Development), and *Training and Development*. He has appeared on the CBS television network's *The Early Show*, CNN, NPR, and many other media programs as an advocate for education reform.

Edward E. Gordon earned his BA and MA in history at DePaul University, Chicago, and his PhD in history and education psychology at Loyola University, Chicago.